THE LAW AND FINANCE OF CORPORATE INSIDER TRADING: THEORY AND EVIDENCE

THE LAW AND FINANCE OF CORPORATE INSIDER TRADING: THEORY AND EVIDENCE

Nasser Arshadi

Thomas H. Eyssell

University of Missouri — St. Louis

Kluwer Academic Publishers
Boston/Dordrecht/London

Distributors for North America:
Kluwer Academic Publishers
101 Philip Drive
Assinippi Park
Norwell, Massachusetts 02061 USA

Distributors for all other countries:
Kluwer Academic Publishers Group
Distribution Centre
Post Office Box 322
3300 AH Dordrecht, THE NETHERLANDS

Library of Congress Cataloging-in-Publication Data
Arshadi, Nasser.
The law and finance of corporate insider trading: theory and evidence / Nasser Arshadi, Thomas H. Eyssell.
p. cm.
Includes bibliographical references and index.
ISBN 0-7923-9360-0 (HB)
1. Insider trading in securities--Law and legislation--United States.
I. Eyssell, Thomas H. II. Title
KF1073.15A96 1993
346.73'092--dc20
[347.30692] 93-19386
CIP

Printed on acid-free paper.

Printed in the United States of America

TABLE OF CONTENTS

CHAPTER FOUR

CHAPTER FIVE

PREFACE

If you've heard of the popular trade titles, James B. Stewart's *Den of Thieves,* or Jesse Kornbluth's *Highly Confident: The Crime and Punishment of Michael Milken,* then you're familiar with the latest books on the subject of insider trading. By no means scholarly, literature of this nature is increasingly profitable, as is insider trading itself. Our research indicates that, despite six decades of anti-insider trading laws, transactions based upon non-public information have continued without any discernable decline in total volume. Registered insiders have simply abstained from illegal trading under their own names, and outside-insiders have taken greater advantage of nonpublic information. For the most part, it seems a matter of legal semantics. And so, rather than glamorize insider trading, this book argues to decriminalize it.

When we began our investigation, we hardly set out to draw such a conclusion. We simply wanted to examine more closely the role of information, specifically private information, as it affects transactions in the capital markets. Modern development of rigorous theories of asset pricing and market efficiency has begged for empirical research on insider trading. And so we decided to concentrate, both theoretically and empirically, on the issues of insider trading and its effects upon market efficiency, asset pricing, and regulation in a technologically advancing and increasingly global environment.

In this book, we establish a theoretical framework within which we examine the regulation of securities markets and the laws of insider trading. Then, we conduct our empirical tests of the effectiveness of these laws around the incidence of tender offers spanning the 1975-1990 period. Next, we discuss the policy implications of our findings mentioned above. Finally, we critique the previous arguments against insider trading.

Our work is more a synthesis of various bodies of law with theories of finance, primarily because those who transact upon materially nonpublic information do so clearly with an understanding of securities laws and case precedents. Gaining a working knowledge of insider trading laws is noteworthy because, since their initial enactment in the 1930s, a steady passage of amendments and the ongoing evolution of case law have complicated legal matters considerably, and not simply by extending the ban on insider trading to include outsiders, such as investment bankers, attorneys, and accountants.

As such a composite of financial and legal issues, this text may appeal to both academic and practitioner markets in finance and corporate law. Instructors may find it a useful supplement to course materials on corporate finance, capital markets, corporate restructuring, and corporate law. Likewise, the book may serve as reference for business professionals such as lawyers, corporate lobbyists, certified public accountants, legislators (especially those who actively involved in drafting laws governing insider trading), and investment bankers and anyone else party to sensitive transactions which have been or may be construed as illegal insider trading.

No scholarly pursuit is possible in a vacuum. And so we would like to thank all those who contributed to and supported our efforts in this work. We thank Cynthia Campbell (University of Massachusetts-Amherst), Gordon Karels (University of Nebraska-Lincoln), and Donald Fraser (Texas A&M University) for reading the initial outline of the project and providing us with supportive comments. We also thank those who read parts of this book and provided us with suggestions to improve it. This includes Philip Dybvig (Washington University in St. Louis), Louis Ederington (University of Oklahoma), Krishna Palepu (Harvard University), David Rose and Robert Sorensen (University of Missouri-St. Louis), and Robert Thompson (Washington University School of Law). We are indebted to our capable research assistants Shelley Bittle, Mary Kay Caragher, Chung-Li Ku, and Yun-ta Wang and to Nancy Tabor who helped us in preparing the camera-ready text. We are grateful to our friends and families for their support including Diane and Megan Eyssell, Bruno, Nadja and Seymour Katz, Nina and Don Murano, and Kirsten Sandberg. And, last, editors at Kluwer Academic Publishers were always very cordial throughout the project.

THE LAW AND FINANCE OF CORPORATE INSIDER TRADING: THEORY AND EVIDENCE

CHAPTER ONE

INTRODUCTION

In the two-and-one-half decades since the publication of Henry Manne's classic *Insider Trading and the Stock Market* (1966), the attention devoted to insider trading in both the financial press and by regulatory authorities has increased dramatically. Over the same period, the nature of insider trading has changed significantly. The archetypical insider trading case of the mid-1960s is that of *Texas Gulf Sulphur Co.*, in which officers purchased their firm's shares subsequent to an important mineral discovery but before its public announcement. In contrast, recent cases have often involved preannouncement trading in the stocks of takeover targets not only by registered corporate insiders (e.g., officers, directors, and large shareholders) but also by those outside the firm. These *outside-insiders* include investment bankers, attorneys, financial printers, and relatives and acquaintances of those with access to material nonpublic information. As a result, regulatory efforts have shifted partially from attempts to monitor those inside the firm to the difficult task of prosecuting outside-insider trading.

This book presents a theoretical and empirical examination of insider trading. We define insider trading as transactions in the shares of publicly held corporations using material nonpublic information. Information is deemed material and nonpublic when its subsequent release significantly alters the share price. Our investigation includes a synthesis of various bodies of law with that of financial theory. This approach is necessitated by the fact that those who transact based on material nonpublic information clearly do so with the knowledge of securities laws and case precedents. Their transactions are also motivated by the potential for substantial profit in trading before public announcements of events such as tender offers. It is our contention that a thorough analysis of insider trading requires the integration of law and finance.

Chapter two provides a conceptual framework in which we explore the theoretical roles of markets, firms, and publicly held corporations. Since insider trading often occurs in the context of certain events in the domain of publicly held corporations (e.g., takeovers), a discussion of corporate governance is provided to determine both who may have access to material nonpublic information, and their legal rights and responsibilities. This discussion begins with an economic analysis of the formation of markets and firms and proceeds to a discussion of corporate governance, the importance of explicit contracts among parties to the corporation, corporate laws designed to fill the gaps left for unwritten contracts, fiduciary duties involving corporate insiders, and the market for corporate control.

Since insider trading takes place in the context of securities transactions involving corporate insiders, brokers, dealers, investment advisors, and arbitragers (among others), an evaluation of insider trading regulation requires a detailed discussion of the regulatory structure of the securities markets. In Chapter three we examine different aspects of the securities laws, including the Securities Act of 1933, the Securities Exchange Act of 1934, and subsequent amendments. The chapter concludes with a critique of the SEC disclosure rules and their ramifications for market efficiency.

Chapter four provides a detailed chronology of insider trading regulations enacted in the United States since 1934. Particular emphasis is given to the increasingly restrictive nature of insider trading regulation and to the recent acceleration in the severity of prescribed penalties. Laws that have been used effectively in such cases (e.g., RICO) but are not explicitly related to insider trading are discussed. This chapter also includes a discussion of several important court decisions, Supreme Court rulings, and the changing nature of SEC and Department of Justice enforcement activities that have provided the impetus for the increasingly strict regulations.

Chapter five is an overview of the existing empirical literature on insider trading. This body of work is concerned primarily with the characteristics of insider transactions, the timing of these transactions, and the effect(s) of regulatory changes on the actions of registered insiders. While it is perhaps not surprising to find significant methodological improvements over the last three decades, we also provide insights into the evolving nature of insider trading over time.

Chapter six presents empirical evidence on two separate but related phenomena: the insider trading activities of registered traders, or inside-insiders, and the effects of trading by those not employed by the firm, or outside-insiders, over the 1975-1990 period. The latter group is particularly interesting because there is a large amount of anecdotal evidence dealing with its existence, but a correspondingly small amount of empirical evidence. The span of time is suitable for an investigation of insider trading for a number of reasons. First, it presents a period during which a series of increasingly restrictive anti-insider trading laws were passed. Second, over this period there were several court rulings dealing with insider trading, including several by the U.S. Supreme Court. And third, both the SEC and the Department of Justice implemented unprecedented enforcement campaigns against insider trading, which raised public awareness of the phenomenon to new heights.

We evaluate the merit of anti-insider trading laws in Chapter seven. Based on both the theoretical arguments and recent empirical developments, we argue that insider trading laws and enforcement activities by the SEC and the Department of Justice have failed to deter insider trading in the aggregate. We further argue that risk-arbitrage transactions (trading based on costly acquisition of material information regarding corporate events such as tender offers) may fall into the category of outside-insider trading. Such transactions based on material nonpublic information (e.g., the case of Ivan Boesky) may violate existing laws. We conclude our discussion by proposing the decriminalization of insider trading.

CHAPTER TWO

MARKETS, FIRMS, AND PUBLICLY HELD CORPORATIONS

If owners of factors of production could exchange their goods in the market without incurring marketing or transaction costs, they would do so without the need to establish a firm. Transaction costs are defined as "search and information costs, bargaining and decision costs, policing and enforcement costs" (Dahlman 1979). The Coase Theorem presents this frictionless market model as a means of demonstrating how positive transaction costs create appropriate incentives for the owners of factors of production to organize themselves within a firm (Coase 1937, 1960, 1988).

The organized stock exchanges, commodity exchanges, and futures and options exchanges are all examples of modern markets. The organizers of these markets set up rules and regulations (apart from governmental regulations) to determine the time of trading, the instruments to be traded, and the parties involved in trading. These rules are designed to reduce transaction costs.

If the transaction costs of multiple exchanges within the firm are less than the cost of carrying out such transactions in the market, the owners of factors of production have an incentive to form a firm. The optimal size for the firm is attained when the transactions cost of the marginal factor of production included in the firm equals the cost of carrying out that transaction in the market.

Firms are organized as composites of voluntary contracts among the owners of the factors of production. This includes those who supply the financial capital necessary for the acquisition of means of production and those who provide human capital and specialized skills required to transform input products into output products. The ownership structures in such firms are determined through minimization of the transaction costs. The emerging forms (proprietorships, partnerships, or corporations) provide the least costly production processes that can survive in a competitive market.

In proprietorships the joining of decision-making responsibilities with risk-bearing responsibilities through the investment of wealth removes the conflict of interest between professional managers and the owners of the firm. Partnerships are suitable for lines of businesses in which the most important source of input is human capital. Transaction costs due to conflicts of interest are minimized when skilled employees mutually monitor each other. However, there are limitations to these structures. Firms that require substantial amounts of capital, a diversity of managerial skills, and the undertaking of large firm-specific risks are organized as open corporations (Fama and Jensen, 1983a and 1983b).

Explicit and voluntary contracts written among the various parties to the corporation (including managers, stockholders, and bondholders) specify many aspects of the expected future conduct of the contracting parties. For example, management compensation plans may spell out payout based on the performance of stock prices, and bond indentures may set limitations on dividend payments to stockholders. But not all future eventualities can be predicted and written into contracts, *ex ante*. Explicit contracts are costly to write and, therefore, must be justified economically.

Beyond specific contracts written by various parties to the corporation, other more general terms included in corporate law are applicable to all corporations because of the broad nature of their provisions. Corporate laws are established as a means of reducing the transactions costs inherent in the writing of explicit contracts in individual firms. Since explicit contracts are costly to develop, some firms may not expend an optimal amount of resources in forming the needed contracts based on the presumptions that other firms who face similar circumstances may develop the format that in return can be copied free of cost. This free-rider problem creates disincentives in developing full-scale contracts. Corporate laws resolve the free rider problem by specifying most general aspects of corporate contracts so that the individual firms will have no need to cover these provisions themselves. Examples of contracts written into corporate law include limited liability of shareholders, voting rights, establishment of the board of directors, fiduciary principles, and the like.

Corporate Governance

One of the important mechanisms established through corporate law is an internal control system to monitor management activities. This function is primarily the domain of a board of directors composed of three or more individuals. The role of the board is specified in the legal requirements of the state chartering authorities. The Model Business

Corporation Act sets forth the following guideline for the board of directors: "All corporate powers shall be exercised by or under authority of, and the business affairs of a corporation shall be managed under the direction of a board of directors."[1] And "[t]he fundamental responsibility of the individual corporate director is to represent the interests of the shareholders as a group, as the owners of the enterprise, in dealing with the business and affairs of the corporation within the law."[2] Directors are, therefore, fiduciaries who owe a duty of loyalty to the shareholders and a duty of care to the corporation.

The standard by which duty of care is measured is called the business judgment rule, which suggests that "[a]bsent bad faith or some other corrupt motive, directors are normally not liable to the corporation for mistakes of judgment, whether those mistakes are classified as mistakes of fact or mistakes of law" (Manne 1967). Thus, in practice, the rule serves more as a standard of judicial restraint to prevent courts from interfering in the activities of corporate directors and managers than as a restrictive duty imposed on directors and managers. The widespread application of the business judgment rule implies that management and board actions may not be reviewed at all (Gilson 1986, p. 741).

In contrast to the judicial restraint under the business judgment rule, courts have taken an active role in transactions that create conflicts of interest and threaten to breach the duty of loyalty. Directors' votes on matters related to their own business relationships with the firm are reviewed and scrutinized by the court to ensure the fairness of the decision. The fairness standard, however, has been shown to be inadequate to discharge the duty of loyalty in extreme circumstances such as a change in control due to an outside takeover (Gilson 1986, p. 742). In sum, when the self-interest of the board members is at issue, the guidance of the business judgment rule and the fairness standard do not guarantee a value-maximizing decision for the shareholders by the directors.

There is some empirical support for the effectiveness of the board of directors in disciplining managers when the board is composed of a significant number of outside directors (Weisback 1988). It has also been shown that the existence of shareholders who control large share blocks

---

[1]American Bar Association, *Corporate Director's Guidebook*, 1978, p. 37.

[2]Supra note 1, p. 12.

may provide an effective control mechanism (Shleifer and Vishny 1986; Agrawal and Mandelker 1990). Brickley, Lease, and Smith (1988) find similar results on the monitoring role of large blockholders except when the blockholder is an institution such as a bank or an insurance company that has a significant business relationship with the current management. Warner, Watts, and Wruck (1988) also find evidence that links management replacements to board monitoring, involvement by large blockholders, and competition among top managers. DeAngelo and DeAngelo (1989) examine the consequences of sixty proxy contests for board representation during 1978—1985 and find that proxy contests are often followed by managerial resignations even when the dissidents are unable to obtain a majority on the board. They report that only one-fifth of firms in their sample had the same management three years after a proxy contest.

Bond covenants are also used to reduce incentive problems within firms. Smith and Warner (1979) document the influence of bond covenants on managerial decisions regarding investment/financing strategies. While their work deals primarily with stockholder-bondholder conflict, they acknowledge that the "contracts comprising the firms are interdependent and simultaneously determined," including those with the management. Similarly, Gilson (1988) has discussed cases in which the creditors of firms with poor performance are involved in removal of top managers.

Morck, Shleifer, and Vishny (1988) examine the relationship between management and board ownership and market valuation of the firm as measured by Tobin's Q. They find evidence of a significant nonmonotonic relationship where Tobin's Q rises as the ownership increases from 0% to 5%, falls as ownership rises from 5% to 25%, and then rises again as the ownership increases beyond the 25% level. They conjecture that the initial rise in the Tobin's Q may not be totally due to the convergence of interests between managers and shareholders. This may be due to stock bonuses provided to management as rewards for high performance. The mid-range ownership that is correlated with the decline in Tobin's Q may reflect entrenchment in cases in which a founding family is part of the board. They suggest that the positive link between ownership stakes of greater than 25% and Tobin's Q reflects the actual convergence of interests between managers and shareholders. These results are also consistent for the ownership by top officers and outside board members.

Finally, other forms of internal discipline over managerial actions include establishment of franchising as opposed to a centralized monitoring of geographically dispersed operations (e.g., Klein 1980; Brickley and Dark 1987), contractual provisions and organizational structures capable of controlling managerial incentive problems (Mayers and Smith 1981 and 1987), and the use of compensation and managerial labor contracts to induce the convergence of interests between management and shareholders (Fama 1980, Jensen and Zimmerman 1985, and Baker, Jensen, and Murphy 1988).

To the extent that the internal control mechanism resolves managerial incentive problems no additional control system is needed. There is, however, evidence to show that internal systems do not fully mitigate managerial incentive problems (Herman 1981). This problem was evident as early as 1932 when Berle and Means discussed the incentive problems inherent in separation of ownership and control within open corporations.

> Those who control the destinies of the typical modern corporation own so insignificant a fraction of the company's stock that the returns from running the corporation profitably accrue to them in only a very minor degree. The stockholders, on the other hand, to whom the profits of the corporation go, cannot be motivated by those profits to a more efficient use of the property, since they have surrendered all disposition of it to those in control of the enterprise.[3]

Under such circumstances an external control mechanism in the form of a market for corporate control may provide the necessary solution.

The Market for Corporate Control

Manne (1965) suggests that the firms most likely to be acquired will be those most requiring improvement. That is, the market for corporate control serves, in part, as an extension of the managerial labor market. Given this orientation, we focus on one important method of effecting a change in control that does not require the consent of incumbent management: the tender offer. In 1979 the SEC provided the following guidelines to legally identify a transaction as tender offer (Ratner 1988, p. 110):

---

[3]Berle and Means (1932), pp. 8—9.

1. The offer is made to more than ten shareholders,
2. The offer is announced publicly,
3. It involves at least five percent of a class of securities,
4 The offer is nonnegotiable,
5. The tender price exceeds the market value by at least two dollars or five percent,
6. The offer involves a limited time frame for consideration (approximately 45 days).

From a financial viewpoint, a crucial consideration in the evaluation of the tender offer as a means of effecting a change in control is the impact on the wealth of the contracting parties, including (but not limited to) target firm stockholders, bondholders, top-level managers, employees, acquiring firm stockholders, and taxpayers. Therefore, to make a sound judgment on whether tender offers are good or bad we must examine the wealth consequences for the parties involved.

Jarrell, et al. (1988) estimate the premiums paid in 663 successful tender offers from 1962—1985 and find that they averaged 19 percent in the 1960s, 35 percent in the 1970s, and 30 percent in 1980s. These figures are consistent with the findings of thirteen other studies of pre-1980 data summarized in Jensen and Ruback (1983). The Office of the Chief Economist of the SEC estimates that in the period 1981—1986 the shareholders of target firms in successful tender offers received premiums in excess of $54 billion over the value of their pre-tender offer share prices. Thus, there is virtual unanimity in the conclusion that target firm shareholders profit from successful tender offers.

Dennis and McConnell (1986) examine the impact of merger bids on the value of target firm bonds (as well as common stock) and conclude that while some classes of creditors (e.g., convertible bondholders) enjoy significant wealth gains, the holders of straight bonds neither gain or lose. It should be noted, however, that the sample period for this study predates the advent of highly leveraged transactions; as a result, it is difficult to generalize their findings to more recent events. The increasing popularity of LBOs and MBOs in the latter part of the 1980s, along with recent work by Asquith et al. (1989) demonstrating high default rates on the type of debt often used in these transactions, suggests that additional research may be necessary to obtain a clearer picture of the effects of takeover bids on target firm bondholders.

Target firm managers are often ousted as the result of takeover bids. Martin (1986) reports that within three years of a successful takeover bid 64% of the target firms' top three managers departed. Similarly, Walsh

(1988) reports that 59% of the target firms he examined experienced management changes within five years of a merger, compared to 33% for nonmerging firms. Because the samples used in these studies include friendly as well as hostile acquisitions, it is highly probable that a sample composed only of hostile tender offers would provide a higher percentage of managerial turnover upon a successful bid.

The finding that target firm managers are often displaced subsequent to a successful takeover bid is consistent with the argument that the market for corporate control acts as an external mechanism for transferring corporate resources to the hands of those better able to utilize them. Thus, an active takeover market serves as an effective monitoring system over managerial performance. From this, one may infer that an effective deterrent to tender offers is corporate efficiency, which increases share prices and discourages takeover bids.

Brown and Medoff (1988) and Shleifer and Summers (1988) have tested the impact of successful tender offers on the wages and employment of workers. The first study reports that, as a result of mergers consummated in the state of Michigan in 1981—1982, the wages of the combined work force in the state declined by about four percent but total employment rose by about two percent. While their study is based on only one state, it indicates that labor may be far less adversely affected than some antitakeover advocates have contended.

Shleifer and Summers, on the other hand, contend that premiums paid to target firm shareholders and the profits received by the acquirers represent wealth transfers from target firm employees resulting from post-takeover wage concessions. They suggest that the observed wealth effects are primarily due to the breach of existing labor contracts. A casual observation, however, indicates that lower fares and higher levels of resource utilization have followed the takeovers of the last several years. Thus, while some cost savings may be attributable to lower wages and salaries, society as a whole has benefitted from lower fares, more travel, and higher employment.

Tax benefits have long been considered an important source of takeover gains. This may no longer be true. The Tax Reform Act of 1986 reduced the incentives for takeovers by decreasing (1) the acquirer's ability to use the accumulated tax losses of the target firm to reduce its own tax liabilities and (2) the acquirer's ability to step up the basis of depreciable assets without being subjected to the capital gain tax. Auerbach and Reishus (1988) examine 318 successful takeovers that occurred from 1968 to 1983 to study tax benefits due to accumulated losses and credits. They find that tax benefits were not a significant factor in the majority of these transactions.

Empirical evidence on the wealth effects of takeover bids on acquiring firm shareholders is best described as mixed. Jensen and Ruback (1983) conclude that tender offer acquirers earn significant positive returns, while those who acquire through merger earn neither positive nor negative excess returns. Jarrell et al. (1988) summarize more recent evidence and conclude that there is an "apparent secular decline in the gains to successful bidders in tender offers" (p. 53). Magenheim and Mueller (1988) contend that the ambiguity in the empirical evidence may be attributable to methodological differences across studies. They conclude that "one's answer to the question 'are shareholders of acquiring firms better off after an acquisition than they were before?' is sensitive to both the choice of time intervals over which before and after performance is defined and the choice of benchmark against which performance is measured" (p. 190).

Morck, Shleifer, and Vishny (1990) identify three types of acquisitions that show systematically lower and predominantly negative announcement period returns to acquiring firms. These three categories of bad acquisitions include those that cross industry lines (diversification acquisitions), those involving rapidly growing targets, and acquisitions subsequent to a period of poor performance by bidding management. Mitchell and Lehn (1990) present evidence that suggests that the acquirer in a value-reducing acquisition increases the likelihood that it will become a target.

We conclude that takeover bids are, on balance, socially desirable transactions when they involve target firms that are crippled by inefficient management.

Information, Asset Pricing, and the Efficient Market Hypothesis

Publicly held firms' securities are traded on organized exchanges or over-the-counter. The prices fluctuate to reflect the release of new and material information over time. The Efficient Market Hypothesis (EMH) indicates that security prices at any given time reflect all the information publicly available about them. Thus, market efficiency depends on the speed and accuracy of information dissemination.

The prices of financial assets for publicly held firms are a function of both the market value of the existing assets and the present value of future opportunities. While the value of existing assets may be determined without much difficulty, the value of future opportunities constitutes a formidable task. At the core of this problem is the difficulty in identifying what information the market needs to determine the value of future opportunities and what process it uses to accurately estimate the value.

The EMH provided the first well-formulated set of answers to these questions more than two decades ago. The weak-form EMH argues that all information regarding past prices is reflected in the current market price of the securities; therefore, any attempt charting past prices to estimate future changes will be useless. This is an obvious attack on the merit of *technical analysis*. The semi-strong form of the hypothesis contends that current market price of a security reflects not only past price information but also all other publicly available information (e.g., accounting statements, annual reports, and earnings announcements). This implies that *fundamental analysis* is useless.

According to the strong-form of the EMH, market prices reflect not only all publicly available information but also the *material nonpublic or inside information.* Implicit in this argument is the assertion that inside information is either signalled to the market without disclosure of the actual information or used in trading by insiders. Signalling, if credible, affects investor predictions of future opportunities and, therefore, affects the pricing of securities. Trading by insiders can move the prices significantly in the direction that inside information conveys. Since insider trading does not carry the uncertainty attributable to uninformed market trading, the insider's profit is nearly risk-free. Profit opportunities in trading based on inside information refutes the strong form market efficiency because it demonstrates that inside information can provide excess returns.

The early empirical evidence on the weak-form EMH indicated that there was no relationship between rate of return in one period and that in preceding periods (Fama 1970). Similarly, empirical evidence on the semi-strong form of the efficient market hypothesis suggests that public information is not generally useful in predicting short-term changes in prices (see the survey by Malkiel, 1987). The empirical evidence, however, has repeatedly rejected the strong-form EMH by depicting positive excess returns to insider trading (e.g., Seyhun 1986, 1992; Arshadi and Eyssell 1991).

Some of the early findings in support of the weak-form EMH have been questioned. Papers by Leroy and Porter (1981) and Shiller (1981) indicate that variations in stock prices are larger than what changes in expectations regarding dividend changes may explain. Fama and French (1988) study long-term price movements and find large negative correlations in prices over three to five years, inconsistent with early assertions of the theory. Despite these problems, recent empirical studies suggest that while weak-form efficient market hypothesis is not entirely consistent with the evidence, the variations do not "grossly" contradict the hypothesis (Mankiw 1991). For more detail of the state of the literature, see Fama (1991).

Economic Rationality and Corporate Law

We have applied the Coasian paradigm of transaction costs to infer properties of markets, firms, and contracts. Corporate law is a potentially cost-efficient method of establishing a set of general contracts applicable to the contracting parties of all firms. The efficiency of corporate law is contingent upon its consistency with the rules of economic efficiency. Efficiency-oriented firms, markets, and exchanges should reevaluate the schemes of their operations continuously and engage in constructive debates with the regulatory agents (e.g., legislators, enforcement agencies, courts) to rewrite old rules and create new ones. Therefore, if private market sources can establish a set of explicit contracts at a cost lower than what is available through corporate law, deregulation must be considered.

Advancements in information production technology amid the new role assumed by financial intermediaries may provide lower cost solutions to some of the contracting problems that were available previously only through corporate law. If markets are efficient in the weak and semi-strong forms, their ramifications need to be incorporated in the securities regulations and disclosure rules. In the next chapter, we discuss regulatory disclosure rules that have focused on information that is already public. We conclude that there seems to be very little value in this type of disclosure.

While regulated parties (firms, exchanges, and markets) may seek efficiency-related deregulations in certain aspects of corporate law, it is not clear that regulatory agencies would agree with that sentiment. As the theory of regulation suggests, regulators form their own utility functions in the course of their tenure. It is unrealistic to assume that they will willingly vote themselves out of commission through deregulation efforts (e.g., see Peltzman 1976, Posner 1971, and Stigler

1971). The burden, therefore, is with the regulated parties to prove unequivocally that regulation is no longer necessary.

The next chapter provides a detailed account of the growth in securities regulations since the 1930s. At the end of this discussion it will be clear that the weight of today's securities regulations is much heavier than ever before, while the extent of deregulation activities initiated by the regulatory agencies is relatively modest.

CHAPTER THREE

SECURITIES REGULATIONS, MARKET EFFICIENCY, AND THE ROLE OF THE SEC

The principal federal component of corporate law is the regulation of securities transactions through the requirement to disclose information before selling securities or filing registration statements before issuing new securities. This chapter provides a detailed examination of securities regulations enacted in the past six decades, with emphasis on the Securities Act of 1933 and the Securities Exchange Act of 1934. After the initial examination of these acts, we critique existing disclosure rules in light of recent theoretical developments in market efficiency, asset pricing, and information production technology. This chapter does not involve itself with insider trading, which is covered in detail in the next chapter. The objective here is to provide a general examination of the regulatory environment in its totality and to analyze the evolution of the current regulatory framework that includes sanctions against insider trading. It is our contention that a thorough examination of insider trading is not possible without consideration of securities regulations in total.

Securities transactions are subject to both federal and state security laws. These transactions are based on Congress's power to regulate interstate commerce and require transactions to involve the use of any means of transportation and communication in interstate commerce. For example, use of mail or telephone to accomplish any part of the transaction including confirmation of a sale and payment bring the transaction under federal jurisdiction. State commissions can also regulate securities transactions so long as their regulations do not conflict with federal laws. State securities laws, commonly known as blue sky laws, apply to the registration of broker-dealers, registration of securities to be traded in the state, and sanctions against fraudulent activities. State securities laws are diverse, despite attempts to unify their provisions. For example, the Uniform Securities Act (USA), adopted in 1956 and revised in 1985, has been adopted in more than thirty states (Ratner 1988). Federal securities statutes include the following:

1. Securities Act of 1933,
2. Securities Exchange Act of 1934,
3. Public Utility Holding Company Act of 1935,
4. Trust Indenture Act of 1939,
5. Investment Company Act of 1940,
6. Investment Advisers Act of 1940,
7. Securities Investor Protection Act of 1970.

After we provide a brief description of each of these statutes to give an overall impression of the federal securities laws, we turn our attention in more detail to the provisions of the acts of 1933 and 1934.

The *1933 Act* regulates public offerings of new securities by requiring the filing of registration statements and the prohibition of fraudulent or deceptive activities in any offer or sale of these securities. The *1934 Act* extends the disclosure requirements of the 1933 act to securities already traded in the market. The 1934 act also established the SEC and empowered it with the responsibility to enforce the 1933 act, which had been assigned previously to the Federal Trade Commission.

The *Public Utility Holding Company Act of 1935* was enacted to prevent abuses in the financing and operation of electric and gas public utility holding companies. Currently, public utilities account for a small percentage of SEC's function. The *Trust Indenture Act of 1939* imposes standards of responsibility on the indenture trustees of debt securities in excess of $5 million. In September 1987, the SEC recommended to Congress a number of amendments to the Act to enhance conformance with contemporary financing techniques and to set new standards for identifying trustees' conflicts of interest.

The *Investment Company Act of 1940* requires the SEC to oversee public companies involved in securities trading. The composition of management, capital structure, and transactions with directors, officers, and affiliates must be approved by the SEC under this act. The *Investment Advisers Act of 1940* (amended in 1960) established rules of registration and regulation of investment advisers similar to but less comprehensive than those established for broker-dealers under the 1934 act. The *Securities Investor Protection Act of 1970* established the Securities Investor Protection Corporation, which is charged with the supervision of the liquidation of securities firms facing financial distress and the arrangement of payments to customers of those firms.

Securities Act of 1933

The stock market crash of 1929 provided the impetus to enact a broad set of securities regulations. Paramount among these was the Securities Act of 1933. The intent of this 1933 act is to provide a regulatory framework for capital markets that provides safeguards against recurrence of the crash and ensures the efficient functioning of the market. These provisions are based on the argument that an efficient market provides the best incentive for investors to bring their funds into the market.

The 1933 act was designed to prevent fraud in the offering of new securities. When President Roosevelt signed the 1933 act he stated that "every issue of new securities to be sold in interstate commerce shall be accompanied by full publicity and information, and that no essentially important element attending the issue shall be concealed from the buying public."[1] In general, securities laws are designed to provide the disclosure of material information on the companies that seek to raise capital publicly. Furthermore, the laws seek to ensure the flow of timely information to the investment community on the companies whose shares are already publicly held. The 1933 act, which is referred to as a disclosure statute, deals primarily with the offering of new securities. Before the securities are offered publicly the issuer is required to file a registration statement with the SEC consisting of a prospectus that will be provided to every purchaser of the security. The registration statement also provides information and exhibits that need not be furnished to purchasers but are placed in the SEC's files for public inspection.

Section 7 of the 1933 act prescribes the information that needs to be included in the registration statement. The SEC has the authority to decide what kind of information needs to be disclosed in the statement. Furthermore, the SEC has the power to ask for additional information or to permit the omission of certain information for particular set of issues. The main form is Form S-1, prescribed for all offerings for which no other form is required.

---

[1]78 Cong. Rec 2264 (1934) message from President Franklin D. Roosevelt.

Deregulation in the 1933 Act

In March 1982, the SEC adopted an integrated disclosure system that allows for joint disclosure of the requirements of the 1933 and 1934 acts. The new system includes all of the basic disclosure requirements of the 1933 and 1934 acts in a new Regulation S-K. New registration forms S-2 and S-3 were adopted for offerings by issuers already registered under the 1934 act. Form S-2 can be filed by any issuer who has been filing under the 1934 act for at least three years. This form allows the issuer to include in the registration statement and the prospectus a copy of its latest annual report to shareholders and a reference to its latest annual report to the SEC on Form 10-K. Form S-3 can also be used by those with a three-year filing history under the 1934 act to register offerings of senior securities, secondary offerings, certain special offerings, and new offerings of equity securities. This form does not require the issuer to include in its registration statement or prospectus any information about itself other than a reference on Form 10-K to the latest annual report. The justification for the adoption of Forms S-2 and S-3 is that the market already has sufficient information about the issuers; therefore, there is no need for further information dissemination through the registration statement and prospectus.

The registration statement becomes effective twenty days after it is filed with the SEC, after which the issuer can sell its securities to the public. While the SEC has the power to delay or suspend the effectiveness of the registration statement, this power has rarely been used.

In 1982 the SEC adopted Rule 415, which broadened the applicability of shelf registration. This rule allows the issuer to register all the securities they expect to sell in the next two years. Over that period the firm can issue these securities at any time without an additional filing of registration statement with the SEC. This allows the issuer to avoid the delays involved in preparation of a new registration statement at the time of each sale. The rule applies to firms that register on Form S-3 and to continuing offerings such as employee purchase plans.

Under this rule the issuing firm is not required to name an underwriter upon the filing of the registration statement. Once a shelf registration has been filed, investment banking firms may submit bids for the issue. Since no underwriter knows with certainty whose bid will ultimately be chosen, there is no incentive to spend resources to investigate the firm in advance.

If no bids are high enough based on the inside information of the issuer, the offering may be postponed until a later date. But if available bids are adequate, the underwriter with the highest bid will be chosen on the day the offering is completed. This procedure, however, leaves very little time for the underwriter to perform diligent investigation to discover any potentially adverse inside information about the issuer. Booth and Smith (1986) state that issuing firms employ underwriters to certify that prices of new securities are consistent with the inside information. With adverse inside information, however, managers have incentive to lie about the true nature of their inside information.

How then can investors trust the certified price of the new issue? It depends on the credibility of the underwriter which is a function of nonsalvageable reputational capital as well as the loss potential on the reputation if cheating occurs. In certification of the issue, the underwriter has to stake its reputation and subject itself to potential lawsuits under Section 11 of the 1933 Act. The fee charged by the underwriter, therefore, should reflect this uncertainty. The underwriter provides insurance regarding the credibility of the issue and prices the reduced due diligence into their fees. Their fees should also be an increasing function of the issuer's firm-specific risk. These hypotheses have been empirically validated by Blackwell, Marr, and Spivy (1990).

Denis (1991) provides further insights on shelf registration: 1) equity issues through the shelf registration process have a more negative impact on the stock prices than the traditional registration procedure; 2) shelf registration is limited to larger, more well-known firms for which there is little information asymmetry; and 3) shelf registration is more cost efficient than the traditional registration when the issue involves debt securities. This cost efficiency occurs because debt securities are issued more frequently and, as a result, more information is available to the underwriters who can then make a sound bid. Equity financing, in contrast, is more infrequent (equity financing by utilities being a significant exception). This may be the main reason nearly 50% of the utility equity offerings in the 1984—1988 period were registered under Rule 415, in contrast to less than two percent for industrial equity offerings over the same period (p. 193). To the extent that shelf registration exists today, Rule 415 has contributed to market efficiency by providing investors with a less-cumbersome, low-cost registration technique. Rule 415 is especially useful when corporations want to access overseas capital markets outside the requirements of the 1933 act in a fast and timely manner. Shelf registration reduces delays and provides flexibility sufficient to retain large issuers of securities in the United States. Shelf registration relieves the issuing firms from disclosing the inside information through the conventional registration technique. The fee system in the market takes the place of regulation and the market assigns correct prices on such securities. Thus the problem of adverse inside information is resolved, and information is reflected in the securities prices without the intervention of the SEC.

The Securities Exchange Act of 1934

As noted previously, the 1933 act deals primarily with the issuance of new securities, while the Securities Exchange Act of 1934 extends the disclosure doctrine of investor protection to securities already listed on national securities exchanges. In August 1964, the 1934 act was amended to require that disclosure and reporting provisions also apply to equity securities of over-the-counter companies with assets in excess of $1 million and more than 500 shareholders.

Unlike the 1933 act, which focuses on a single provision and has not changed significantly over time, the 1934 act deals with a wide array of issues concerning existing securities, including (1) establishment of the Securities and Exchange Commission; (2) regulation of trading in markets and registration of market participants; (3) regulation of publicly held firms; (4) corporate reporting; (5) rules regarding investigation, enforcement, and statutory sanctions against violations of securities laws; (6) tender offers; and (7) insider trading. The provisions of the 1934 act have been amended several times, most notably in 1964, 1968, 1975, 1984, and 1988.

The Establishment of the Securities and Exchange Commission

The establishment of the Securities and Exchange Commission (SEC) as part of the 1934 act created a powerful agency charged with enforcement and administration of the federal securities laws. The agency consists of five commissioners appointed by the president for five-year terms. The term of one commissioner expires every year and no more than three members can be from the same political party. The SEC employs about 2000 staff members who occupy its main office in

Washington, D.C. as well as nine regional and five branch offices at financial centers across the country.

The main source of the securities law is the statutes. Since statutes are ambiguous, there are two additional sources of law: the rules that SEC issues and case laws that has developed over time. Most of the law related to the 1933 act can be found in the rules, forms, or policy statements of the SEC. In areas related to the 1934 act, however, a great deal of case law interpretation is required (such as the provisions of antifraud statutes). The SEC maintains three sets of rules. The first set includes procedural and technical rules, such as rules prescribing the number of copies to be filed. The second set consists of definitions of terms (e.g., defining what constitutes intrastate offering under Rule 147 of the 1933 act). The third set consists of substantive rules (e.g., the proxy solicitation rule under the 1934 act, Section 14). The SEC is also in charge of determining the content of forms that reporting publicly held corporations, issuers, and broker-dealers have to file with the agency. Financial disclosure plays an important part in the administration and enforcement of the securities laws, and the authority over the content of these forms provides SEC a great regulatory power. Since disclosure requirements impose significant cost on the regulated entities, their economic rationale have been questioned over the years. We will return to this subject later in this chapter.

In addition to issuing rules and forms, the SEC issues opinions on a wide variety of topics through releases. These releases do not constitute legal requirements; nevertheless, they amount to informal law-making. Finally, the SEC responds to individual private inquiries regarding certain transactions through no-action letters, which mean that if the inquiring party follows the recommendations of the SEC there will be no action on behalf of the agency.

Regulation of Exchanges and Markets, and Registration of Market Participants

The 1934 act, as amended, requires the following parties to register with the SEC:

1. national securities exchanges,
2. brokers and dealers who conduct securities transactions in interstate commerce,
3. transfer agents,

4. clearing agencies,
5. municipal brokers and dealers,
6. securities information processors.

Exchanges are self-regulatory organizations. The New York Stock Exchange (NYSE) is the oldest and largest securities exchange in the United States, having existed for 140 years prior to the enactment of the 1934 act. During that period the exchange developed its own set of rules for members to follow, as well as sanctions against those who disobey. Instead of eliminating self-regulation of the exchanges, Congress superimposed the SEC on them as an extra level of regulation. To register with the SEC, the exchanges are required to design rules to "prevent fraudulent and manipulative acts and practices"and "to promote just and equitable principles of trade." These rules should also contain provisions to discipline the members of the exchange if they violate the established regulations. The rules include provisions governing listing and delisting securities on the exchange, obligations of the issuers of the securities, clearing of exchange transactions, the organizational form of the member firms, and qualifications of member firms' partners and officers, among other things. The regulatory responsibility of every member firm is assigned to one exchange. If a firm is a member of the NYSE as well as other exchanges, the regulatory supervision will be with the NYSE. The American Stock Exchange regulates member firms that are not also listed on the NYSE.

Over-the-counter (OTC) securities are traded among security dealers and not organized by exchanges. By an amendment to the 1934 act in 1938, Congress provided for the creation of a self-regulatory organization to take regulatory responsibility for the OTC securities. The National Association of Securities Dealers (NASD) is registered with the SEC and is charged with preventing fraudulent activities and promoting equitable principles of trade among OTC dealers. Prior to 1971, all OTC trading took place by telephone calls between dealers based on published quotations in commercial sheets. In 1971, the Association put into operation an electronic quotation system (NASDAQ) for selected OTC securities. Dealers can insert and update their bid-asked quotations for securities with which they are registered with the NASD as market makers.

The 1934 act also put in place provisions that regulated trading on the securities markets themselves. Sections 7 and 8 regulate margin trading, and Section 11 governs trading by exchange members for their own accounts. In 1975 Congress added Sections 11A and 17A which directed the SEC to establish a national market system and a national system for settlement and clearing of transactions.

Sections 7 and 8 of the 1934 act authorized the Board of Governors of the Federal Reserve System (the Fed) to set limitations on the amount of credit that can be extended for the purpose of purchasing equity securities. The margin trading restrictions apply only to equity securities and set no limits on credit for purchasing U.S. government bonds, state and local government bonds, and nonconvertible corporate bonds. The objective of margin trading regulation is to prevent excessive use of credit for the purchase of securities. While the Fed sets the margin limits, the responsibility for investigating and enforcing the margin rules that relate to broker-dealers belongs to both the SEC and to self-regulatory organizations such as exchanges.

Securities exchanges provide a marketplace in which member firms and brokers can buy and sell stocks on behalf of their clients. Section 11 of the 1934 act is concerned with the trading of exchange members on their own accounts because of possibly unfair advantages they may have over non member customers in trading. The Act as amended focuses on floor and off-floor trading by members, trading by odd-lot dealers, transactions by specialists, block positioning by member firms, and managed institutional accounts. The objective of Section 11(a) of the 1934 Act was to authorize the SEC to establish rules that would regulate or prevent floor trading and prevent excessive off-floor trading by members if it is "detrimental to the maintenance of a fair and orderly market". Prior to the adoption of a rule by the SEC prohibiting floor trading, a small percentage of NYSE members could use the exchange floor to trade only on their own accounts. The 1964 rule prohibited this type of trading unless the exchanges designed plans, approved by the SEC, to require floor traders to register with the exchanges, retain minimum capital, pass a qualifying exam, and comply with certain restrictions in their trading (e.g., NYSE Rules 110—112). Subsequently, in 1978, NYSE Rule 107 established "registered competitive market makers" with responsibilities to assist the specialists in maintaining an orderly market. Most floor traders have now switched to this new category.

Off-floor trading refers to buy and sell orders that are made in the offices of the members outside the exchanges. While these types of trades account for a substantial volume of members' trading, there had been little interference by the SEC until a 1967 study by the

Commission. This prompted the NYSE to prevent member firms from transmitting orders to the exchanges before that of their customers if they had access to "inside information." Despite this rule, it has been revealed that during the stock market crash of 1987, some member firms indeed had transmitted their orders ahead of their customers when they knew that share prices were likely to decline due to large sell orders.

The specialist firm within an exchange functions as a broker's broker by maintaining a book on which brokers can place their customers' limit orders, and as market-maker in assigned stocks by trading with brokers when there are no customer orders on the book to match the trades. With the monopoly trading position and the knowledge of orders in the book, the specialist potentially can make large profits by moving prices of their stocks up and down. Because of the abusive possibility of this arrangement, in 1975 Congress provided the SEC with the authority to limit specialists to act either as brokers or as dealers, but not as both. The SEC has not used this authority to date.

Prior to 1975 there were fixed minimum commission rates maintained by NYSE. This led a substantial portion of institutional trading to shift to regional exchanges and to the establishment of a significant over-the-counter market for NYSE listed stocks, which was maintained by nonmember market makers. This resulted in a situation wherein a single stock could have different prices in different exchanges. In the 1975 amendment (11A) , Congress directed the SEC to facilitate the establishment of a national market system to link all markets for particular securities. Subsequently, in 1976 the old NYSE tape was replaced with a consolidated tape that records all transactions in a listed stock, wherever the transaction takes place. In 1978, an intermarket trading system (ITS) was introduced that allows for electronic transfer of orders from one exchange to another.

The 1934 act defines a broker as a person who trades in securities for the account of others. A dealer is defined as a person who trades in securities for his/her own account. The Investment Advisers Act of 1940 defines an investment adviser as person who advises others for a fee in selection of securities to buy or sell. Brokers and dealers, who are engaged in the interstate securities business, are required to register with the SEC. Under rule 15(b) of the 1934 act, the SEC may revoke or suspend a broker-dealer's license if it is found that the party has violated the securities laws.

Broker-dealers transact in securities using their customers' funds. To safeguard these funds, the broker-dealers are required to meet certain financial requirements, which include minimum capital requirements, segregation of customers' funds and securities, and the maintenance of an industry-wide insurance fund to cover the claims of customers' if their brokerage houses become insolvent. Rule 15c3-1 of the 1934 act requires that a broker-dealer must maintain net capital of at least $25,000 and its aggregate indebtedness may not exceed 1500% of its net capital (800% in the first year).

Customers leave substantial amounts of securities and cash balances with their brokers. This includes securities purchased on margin (and held by brokers as collateral for their loans), fully paid securities (held by brokers for customers as a matter of convenience), and cash balances of customer accounts. In an investigation of the operational crisis of the industry in 1968—1970, investigators found out that not all securities were kept segregated in customers' accounts and brokers did not always have the actual possession of the securities they were supposed to hold for their customers. With regard to cash balances in customer accounts, the standard practice of the industry at the time was to use the cash as a source for a interest free loan. SEC Rule 15c3-3 adopted in 1972 required all brokers to promptly obtain and thereafter maintain the physical possession of all fully paid securities. The rule also required brokers to maintain a Special Reserve Bank Account in which they hold cash or U.S. government securities in amounts equal to cash balances of customers' accounts minus margin loans.

To establish a secure system of customer protection, Congress passed the Securities Investor Protection Act of 1970 (SIPA), which created a nonprofit member corporation —the Securities Investor Protection Corporation (SIPC). Brokers registered with the SEC are required to be members of SIPC. SIPC is managed by a seven-person board of directors who are appointed by the Secretary of Treasury (one person), the Federal Reserve Board (one person), and the President (the remaining five people). To finance the SIPC, the SEC required brokers to pay one-half of one percent of their gross revenues into the fund until it reached $150 million, and to pay further assessments if needed. SIPC (through the SEC) can also borrow up to $1 billion from the U.S. Treasury. The SEC may further impose a charge of not more than two basis points on all transactions on exchanges and over-the-counter markets to provide for repayment on customer accounts.

The general anti-fraud provisions of the securities laws apply to the conduct of business by broker-dealers. There are two areas in which such provisions may be applicable: 1) when there is a conflict of interest between a broker-dealer and the customer and 2) when the broker-dealer has inadequate information about the issuer. The conflict of interest may arise when a customer deals with a broker who also acts as a dealer on certain securities. The legal responsibility of the broker to act in such transactions for the benefit of the customer does not apply to the former's role as a dealer in the securities that they buy from the customer or sell to the customer. However, the court has historically accepted the argument by the SEC that broker-dealers must make full disclosure of their potential conflict of interests with the customer when they operate both as brokers and dealers, otherwise they will be charged with violation of antifraud provisions.[2]

To ensure that broker-dealers make recommendations to their customers based on sound information, the SEC adopted Rule 15c2-11 in 1971. This rule prohibits trade recommendations on any securities unless 1) the issuer has made disclosures based on a recent offering under the 1933 act, 2) the issuer has been filing reports under the 1934 act, or 3) the broker-dealer has in its files current financial information about the issuer.

Regulation of Publicly Traded Corporations

Sections 12, 13, 14, and 16 of the 1934 act regulate the operation of publicly held corporations. Section 12 requires publicly traded securities to be registered with the SEC. Section 13 requires all securities that are registered under Section 12 to file periodic financial reports with the SEC. Section 14 regulates the solicitation of proxies from security holders. Section 16 requires directors, officers, and owners of 10% or more of the equity shares of publicly held companies (registered insiders) to report to the SEC their holdings of company securities upon their designation as registered insiders. This section also requires the registered insiders to file any subsequent changes in their holdings at the end of the month in which the transaction has occurred.

Under Section 13 of the 1934 act corporations are required to file their basic reports including the annual report (Form 10-K), the quarterly report (Form 10-Q), and the current report (Form 8-K) that is filed monthly if unscheduled material or events need to be filed with the SEC.

---

[2]Charles Hughes & Co. v. SEC, 139 F.2d 434 (2d Cir. 1943).

These filings contain an extensive array of information. Form 10-K contains the following:

1. the main business of the company,
2. the location of principal properties,
3. the brief description of material legal proceedings pending,
4. identification of registered insiders along with the percentage and the amount of their holdings in corporate securities,
5. the principal market in which voting securities are traded and the frequency and amount of dividends paid in the last two years and plans for future dividends,
6. five-year selected data such as sales, income or loss, total assets, long-term obligations and the effects of inflation on such figures,
7. management's analysis of financial conditions such as liquidity, capital resources, and favorable and unfavorable trends,
8. two-year audited balance sheets and three-year audited statements of income and changes in financial condition,
9. information on directors and executive officers including name, office, and term of office,
10. a list of directors and three highest paid officers (a June 1992 proposal by the SEC attempts to overhaul the way companies report their executive payroll. This includes a requirement to list the five highest paid executives' exact salary, bonus, options, and restricted stocks),
11. a complete, audited annual financial information and any unscheduled material filed in an 8-K during the year.

Form 10-Q repeats most of the disclosure requirements of Form 10-K and requires the following items:

1. income statement,
2. balance sheet,
3. sources and uses of funds,
4.a narrative of material changes in the amount of revenues and expenses in relation to previous quarters,
5. material legal proceedings pending,
6. material changes in the rights of holders of registered securities,

7. withdrawal or substitutions of assets that are used as collateral for any registered securities,
8. any defaults on payments of principal, interest sinking fund or dividend not cured within 30 days,
9. increase in amounts of new issues, continuous issues, or reissues of securities with a statement of purpose,
10. decrease in amounts of securities,
11. information concerning shareholders meetings,
12. other important events for shareholders not included earlier

Form 8-K provides a report of the unscheduled material events that are important to the shareholders and to the SEC including:

1. changes in control of the registrant,
2. acquisition or disposition of assets,
3. bankruptcy or receivership,
4. changes in certifying accountant,
5. financial statements and exhibits,
6. resignations of directors,
7. other materially important events

Section 14 of the 1934 Act relates to proxy solicitations for events that require shareholder vote. This section requires the registered company to provide a proxy statement to each shareholder containing information specified in Schedule 14A along with a form that asks the shareholder to vote yes or no on the proposal expected to be voted upon in the next meeting. The 1934 act requires shareholders to file a proxy statement with the SEC at least ten days before they are sent to security holders. For instance, a private conversation of employees or shareholders regarding a critique of the management performance would trigger a proxy filing. This has long been criticized by the shareholder groups as too restrictive of their right to exchange information.

The June 1992 proposal by the SEC provides for a sweeping change in proxy rules. At the heart of the proposed change is how much input the shareholders should have in a company's direction and how accountable the management should be to its security holders. The proposal seeks to free shareholders in expressing their views on the direction of the firm's operation through exchange of information with other shareholders without having to meet the arcane requirements of the original act. Under the proposal shareholders may meet and discuss how they want to vote in an upcoming meeting without filing a statement with the SEC unless they own 5% or more of the shares as a group. Any written material sent to other shareholders still needs to be filed with the SEC but now it can be done after it is sent to shareholders. Any communication by phone is excluded from the proposed rule because it would allow large institutional investors to secretly exchange information. Another aspect of the proposal is to allow the dissident shareholders to include their nominees with the names of management nominees on their ballots. Currently, the dissidents are alone on their ballots while the management-backed directors have the full slate, which gives voters the choice of either voting for the single dissident or for the management slate. Finally, the proposal requires companies to unbundle related proposals so that they can be voted upon separately.

Regulation of Tender Offers

In 1968 Congress amended the Securities Exchange Act of 1934 with the objective of protecting the interests of shareholders when there is a change in corporate control. Known as the Williams Act, the amendment requires acquirers to publicly disclose certain information, which is specified in Sections 13(d) and 14(d, e), to assure shareholders of an informed decision-making process during a tender offer.[3]

The main objective of Section 13 is to inform the shareholders of the acquisition of a significant block (five percent or more) of the outstanding shares by an outside individual or firm. Section 13(d) stipulates that within ten days of share acquisition, the following information must be disclosed: 1) the identity and background of the purchaser, 2) the source and amount of funds spent on the acquisition, 3) the number of shares owned, and 4) the intentions of the acquirer (investment, takeover, etc.), 5) any planned changes in the event of a successful takeover.

The rules of Section 13 pertain to virtually any initial acquisition of five percent or more of a firm's outstanding shares, and to subsequent

---

[3]The 1968 Williams Act (Pub. L. No. 90-439, 82 Stat. 454 July 29, 1968) and 1970 Amendments (Pub. L. No. 91-567, 84 Stat. 1497 December 22, 1970). It was specified in the Williams Act that the attempted acquisition must involve at least ten percent of the securities. The 1970 amendment reduced the triggering proportion to five percent.

acquisitions of two percent or more. On the other hand, Section 14(d) of the act deals specifically with the acquisition of shares via tender offer. Under this Section, share purchasers must file form 14d-1 with the Securities and Exchange Commission, which entails disclosure of information similar to that listed above. Additionally, it allows sellers the opportunity to change their minds within sixty days of an offer, or to withdraw their shares if they are misinformed. Further, all holders in the target class of securities must receive the same offer, and if the offer price is raised by the acquirer, the new price also applies to shareholders who have already sold their shares. Section 14(e) requires the management of the target company to provide shareholders with a statement of the company's position on the tender offer and the reasons for the position within ten days of the tender offer. This Section also makes it unlawful for either the bidder or target management to attempt to deceive shareholders or manipulate share prices during the offer.

The extension of the SEC's enforcement power to tender offers has been considered by some courts, primarily in the event of fraud or deception on the parts of bidder or the target. The Supreme Court has ruled, for example, that bidders may not sue for damages when misleading statements are made by the management of target companies.[4] Shareholders may initiate a civil suit if they are misled by those who make the tender offer.[5] And the target firm's management cannot be sued by shareholders if a tender offer is abandoned as a result of misleading statements made by the former.[6] While these precedents are not necessarily clear cut and will perhaps change in the future, they nevertheless present a judiciary sentiment that is generally sympathetic to the target firm's management.

In addition to the federal regulation of tender offers through the Williams Act, tender offers are also subject to regulation by the state, which often imposes greater restrictions. Required delays between public announcements and the commencement of tender offers (sometimes as long as sixty days) are not uncommon in state law. The criteria for

---

[4]Piper V. Chris-Craft Industries, 430 U.S. 1 (1977).

[5]Plaine v. McCabe, 797 F. 2d 713 (9th Cir. 1986).

[6]Lewis v. McGraw, 619 F. 2d 192 (2d Cir. 1980); Panter v. Marshall Field, 646 F. 2d 271 (7th Cir. 1981).

disclosure are also typically more expansive than SEC provisions. In addition, administrative review hearings for tender offers have been established in several states.

Empirical evidence on the effects of state and federal regulation changes on takeover premiums is somewhat mixed. Data suggesting that the first generation of state takeover laws may have had the effect of deterring some bidders is reported by Smiley (1981). And Jarrell and Bradley (1980) conclude that the first-generation state laws and the Williams Act significantly increased the premiums paid to the shareholders of target firms. On the other hand, recent work by Nathan and O'Keefe (1989) suggests that average tender offer premiums in cash tender offers rose significantly in 1974, possibly due to "events such as the oil crises and subsequent unexpected inflation [which] increased the heterogeneity of investors' beliefs about firm value" (p. 119). Further, Franks and Harris (1989) report increases in takeover premiums for mergers in the United Kingdom after 1968, which suggests that the passage of the Williams Act may have been a coincident, rather than causal, event.

In 1982 the U.S. Supreme Court decision ruled the Illinois tender offer statute unconstitutional in *Edgar v. Mite Corp.* (457 U.S. 624, 1982). This decision helped to create the environment necessary for the passage of a second generation of state laws designed to pass the constitutional test set by the Supreme Court. A wave of second-generation state laws were passed, many of which were upheld by the Court.[7]

The shareholders of target firms may suffer when anti-takeover legislation is passed. Ryngaert and Netter (1987), for example, report that, upon the passage of anti-takeover laws in Ohio, the stock prices of firms incorporated in the state declined by 3.24%, on average.

Investigation, Enforcement, and Statutory Sanctions

The SEC is authorized by law to enforce the provisions of the 1933 and 1934 acts. This part of the SEC's task is conducted by regional offices and the Division of Enforcement. Investors' inquiries and

---

[7]Including Arizona, Florida, Indiana, Louisiana, Maryland, Massachusetts, Minnesota, Missouri, Nevada, North Carolina, Ohio, Oregon, Pennsylvania, Utah, Washington, and Wisconsin.

complaints provide important sources of leads to detect violations of the securities laws. SEC investigators also pay unannounced visits to the offices of the brokerage houses and securities dealers to examine whether their conduct is consistent with SEC rules. Unusual movements in stock prices can also provide the SEC the initial tip on possible wrongdoing.

There are several categories of securities violations. First, violations may take place due to filing false information in registration statements or selling securities without registrations. Second, any misrepresentation of the facts or intentional omissions may violate the anti-fraud rules. Third, manipulation of stock prices is also illegal.

The statutory sanctions available to the SEC include civil injunction, criminal prosecution, and administrative remedy. Historically, the SEC had to wait for a criminal conviction before it could bring civil lawsuits against the violations of the securities laws. In 1984, the Insider Trading Sanctions Act provided the authority to the SEC to bring such suits without a criminal conviction. Criminal prosecution is conducted if there is fraud or willful law violations. The SEC refers the facts to the Department of Justice with a recommendation for criminal prosecution. Administrative remedies are also available for the SEC to use when brokers and dealers violate the securities laws. Since these parties have to register with the SEC, their licenses may be revoked either permanently or temporarily depending upon the seriousness of the charges.

A Critique of the SEC's Performance

What Are the Objectives of the Disclosure Requirements?

There are two stated objectives for enactment of the 1933 and 1934 acts: 1) to provide for a disclosure system that will help investors make informed choices and 2) to prevent fraud.

Since its inception, the SEC has required disclosure of historical information about past performance. It has, to a large extent, discouraged the release of soft information, with the exception of Rule 175 passed in 1979. The safe harbor provision of the rule allows for the projection of future prospects, provided that they are linked to past factual information. While safe harbor for projection provides an opportunity for the disclosure of soft information, a significant portion of the relevant information regarding the future prospects of the firm is left to the market because the SEC neither requires nor penalizes the disclosure of such information. Thus, this policy is clearly backward looking, providing very little material information for investors.

There are signs that the SEC may be ready to implement some elements of market-value accounting. Long criticized for shortcomings in the historical accounting disclosures, the Financial Accounting Standards Board (FASB) recently released a compromise version of a proposal to require marking-to-market of corporate assets. The impetus for such a proposal, which is backed by the SEC, is the inability of historical accounting disclosures to uncover substantial losses in the savings and loan associations and commercial banks. The crisis in the savings and loan industry has led to the failure of one-third of the institutions and financial distress of at least another one-third of the industry. With the historical cost disclosure system, failing S&Ls could cover up their losses and continue the practice of arbitraging the federal deposit insurance agencies, ultimately costing the taxpayers several hundred billion dollars in bailout efforts. The only way regulators could detect financial distress was through direct examination of the institution. As the number of insolvent institutions increased, the time between bank examinations was extended, leading to greater losses.

Proponents of historical cost disclosures (e.g., Easterbrook and Fischel 1991) provide the following three reasons for their support. First, historical cost reporting provides objective and uniform information, enabling intraindustry comparisons. In the absence of a uniform disclosure system based on historical cost, firms will have incentives to disclose only information that is sufficiently unusual, making any meaningful comparisons within the industry difficult. Second, historical cost disclosure makes legal enforcement of the disclosure rules more effective, since the requirement is to disclose only objective easy-to-prove historical facts rather than a series of speculative statements regarding future prospects. This provides for a low-cost litigation process because investors are exposed to the same sets of information, enabling the litigants to bring class-action suits. The third advantage of historical disclosure is that standardized disclosure is a federal law. This precludes the incentive problems in the state disclosure requirement and fraud rules that may favor the residents of one state over the other. Since most securities are traded across state lines, a federal law governing disclosure rules set up by a federal agency (e.g., the SEC) is better able to enforce uniform rules.

A Critique of the Current System

The Efficient Market Hypothesis (EMH) states that market prices of securities reflect all available information regarding a given security. As noted previously, the empirical evidence on the EMH generally supports the weak and semi-strong forms of market efficiency, suggesting that publicly available information is reflected in the current market price. With respect to the current discussion, the implication of this theory is that disclosure of historical facts in the form of accounting information cannot provide any material information to shareholders because such information has already been disseminated in the market through news announcements, sales reports, inventory orders, mergers, divestitures, spinoffs, and the like. This point has had its sympathizers even within the SEC. In 1972, William J. Casey, then Chairman of the SEC, made the following remarks regarding the issue (Casey, 1972, pp. 33—34):

> I am . . . unhappy with the content of the contemporary prospectus. . . We all know that the securities markets are essentially markets for discounted future incomes and that investors are future oriented. The disclosure system exists to help investors. Yet as now administered, it does so in a strange way by blocking out . . . any reference to the matters in which investors are most keenly interested. Projections of future earnings are one example. Actual market values of assets carried at depreciated historical cost are another.
>
> The traditional view does not even permit-let alone require-that we sully the purity of a prospectus by references to these earthy subjects. Of course, these forbidden topics always come up in the actual sale of securities. Everybody talks about them. But you can seldom print anything about them in a prospectus or a proxy statement. Why? Some say that the investor must make up his own mind about these vital topics, that the prospectus can only supply him with raw and rather unpalatable factual material that he must sift for himself. Others say that investors are so stupid that they would attach undue weight to forecasts and appraisals. Somehow this applies only to forecasts and appraisals found in documents filed under the securities laws. Forecasts and appraisals appearing in the *New York Times* or in the *Wall Street Journal* are okay. This investors-are-stupid theory seems hard to square with the every-man-his-own-analyst rationale. Yet there

> are intelligent men who subscribe to both theories simultaneously. Despite Casey's arguments, future-oriented information has yet to become part of the required disclosures.

It is instructive to note that share prices of equity securities are a function of both the existing assets and the present value of growth opportunities (PVGO). Accounting information disclosed to the SEC provides at best some information about the value of the existing assets, and disregards almost totally the PVGO. On the disclosure of the value of the existing assets, the information is dated, reflecting the historical cost of the existing assets as opposed to their replacement cost or the market values. More recent proposals by the FASB may improve the accounting of the existing assets to the extent that the reported data is marked-to-market. PVGO, however, is absent from the disclosed information.

Share prices often change when new information is released regarding future prospects, embodied in the PVGO. Firms that have insignificant amounts of PVGOs (low growth firms such as utilities) have share prices that do not vary much over time. To the extent that accounting information provides possible patterns of future growth (related to past growth), prices reflect that information. This price, however, cannot predict future changes in prices; therefore, disclosure does not help investors make better choices regarding their investments.

Developments in asset pricing models (Capital Asset Pricing Model (CAPM) in the mid-1960s and the Arbitrage Pricing Model (APT) in the 1970s) have provided many insights into the type of information that is relevant in asset pricing. Both models rely heavily on non-firm-specific information to determine prices. The one-factor CAPM estimates the expected stock return based on the market risk of the stock, which is influenced primarily by macroeconomic factors with total exclusion of the firm-specific information. The multi-factor APT model computes the expected return based on several factors including market, industry, and other variables that are exogenous to the firm. The crucial implication of these models is that diversified investors should have little interest in the kind of information that the SEC requires in the disclosure forms.

The impact of the securities regulations and disclosure requirements have been tested empirically. Stigler (1964) and Jarrell (1981) have examined whether mandated disclosure requirements of the 1933 act increased the average return earned by new-issue investors. Neither of these studies found any significant increase in average returns following the disclosure requirements. Both concluded that the federal regulation of new-issues markets was ineffective. Benston (1973) examined the effects of the formal reporting requirements of the 1934 act. He focused on the requirement to disclose sales data and concluded that the requirements of the 1934 act had no measurable positive effect on NYSE listed stocks. Simon (1989), however, contends that the effects of disclosure requirements cannot be measured solely by average returns because the existence of uncertainty about a security in the absence of disclosure requirements need not imply that the security is overvalued or undervalued. According to this argument, if disclosure requirements provide quality information to investors, the riskiness of investors' purchases should decline. Her results indicate that 1) investors in seasoned securities and those listed in the NYSE earned normal risk-adjusted returns both before and after the securities regulations; 2) unseasoned issues listed in non-NYSE exchanges earned significantly greater risk-adjusted returns since the securities regulations; and 3) the dispersion of abnormal returns for all issues (seasoned and unseasoned, NYSE and non-NYSE stocks) is significantly lower following the securities act. She attributes the reduction in investor error to post-disclosure improvements in the quantity and quality of available financial information.

Simon's findings help in refocusing the debate. For NYSE-listed issues there is no evidence of mispricing before or after the enactment of the securities regulations. The risk, however, is reduced in the post-regulation period. If the main objectives of the securities regulations were to prevent fraud and to provide sufficient information to investors to make informed decisions, then these findings do not justify the regulation as long as there is no case of overvaluation or undervaluation of the securities. Investors' expectations should be unbiased in both pre- and post-regulation periods. In the case of non-NYSE listed issues, the findings suggest that there is a significant increase in the risk-adjusted returns in the post-regulation period. Does this result justify disclosure requirements imposed on this class of issues? Considering the existing state of information technology it is not clear if the task perceived to be performed by public authorities could not have been accomplished by purely private market sources. We turn to this discussion next.

Information Production Through Market Sources Without Legal Intervention

In the absence of disclosure requirements would purely private market sources produce the optimal amount of quality information? There are two points to be made in support of a private market source for information production. First, private-market disclosures before the 1930s regulations provide a glimpse of a market for information without legal intervention. Second, the technological advancements in information production provide potentially powerful alternatives to regulatory disclosures.

Disclosure requirements apply to four groups of securities: 1) seasoned stocks listed in large exchanges; 2) unseasoned stocks of companies listed in the NYSE; 3) initial public offerings (IPOs); and 4) securities listed in regional exchanges. Information on seasoned securities that are listed on the NYSE is available through past corporate performance and the securities trading history compiled by the NYSE. Information on unseasoned securities of the listed firms are produced by underwriters and brokers and are collected by the NYSE. Prior to the securities acts, the NYSE gathered and processed financial information on its listed securities. The decision to list a security also provided the financial community a signal that the listed company was willing to supply a sufficient amount of quality information. Hilke (1984) provides a chronology of disclosure requirements of the NYSE: the NYSE's Committee on Stock List required disclosure of financial conditions (1869); firms to submit Statement of Condition and list of corporate officers (1870-1880); listing on the exchange (1910); initial offering disclosure reports (1910); quarterly earnings statements (1924); establishment of depreciation policies (1927); requirement of independent audits (1928); and the listing agreement including pledge to supply any reasonable information required by the exchange (1930). This list is so comprehensive, it is difficult to find any significant disclosure requirement in the securities regulations of the 1930s that had not been previously required by the NYSE.

In the case of IPOs, an unregulated market may encourage sellers of securities to cheat in the information provided to buyers. This incentive problem, however, can be mitigated, at least partially, by the loss of repeat business and reduction in the value of reputational capital. While repeat sales may not fully mitigate fraud (Klein and Leffler, 1981), investment in nonsalvageable, firm-specific capital would make short-term profits from cheating less valuable than the long-term cost of lost business.

In IPO transactions there are two sets of incentive problems: the problem between informed seller and uninformed buyer and the incentive problems between an issuer of a security and the investment banker. Empirical investigation of new-issue offerings show that an average issue is offered at a significant discount from the price in the after-market (see Ibbotson 1975, Ibbotson and Jaffe 1975, Ritter 1984, 1985; and Chalk and Peavy 1985.) The hypothesis that repeat business and the value of reputational capital provides the incentives for investment bankers to produce optimal amounts of information about a new issue is tested by Beaty and Ritter (1987). They contend that there is an equilibrium amount of underpricing. If an investment banker underprices too much, the banker will lose on future sales of potential issuers. Conversely, if the banker underprices too little he will lose investor business. They examine investment banking firms with highest and lowest average deviations from their estimated normal underpricing during the period 1977--1981. For those with greatest deviation, the market share declines from 46.6% to 24.5%, while firms with smallest deviation have declines from 27.2% to 21%. These results imply that a purely private market mechanism may, in the long-run, provide appropriate incentives for the issuer as well as the investment banker to produce the optimal amount of credible information even in the absence of securities regulations.

One of the arguments provided by early proponents of securities regulations and the establishment of the SEC was that the free-market system left to its own devices may not produce a socially optimal amount of information. Among the impediments to the free-market information was the public goods characteristic of information: Low resale costs and the free-rider problem may prevent private producers of information from receiving the appropriate price for the information produced. Therefore, the market for private information production would self-destruct.

The problem, however, does not seem to be all that significant in the presence of modern financial intermediaries. Investment and commercial banking firms have developed credible third-party information processing systems that provide the appropriate information to the market. It has been argued theoretically (Fama 1985) and empirically (James 1987, Mikkelson and Partch 1986) that announcements of bank credit agreements with their corporate clientele result in significant price reactions in corporate stock. While corporate customers often directly finance their needed capital in the capital market, they often use commercial banks as credible third-party rating agencies that provide reliable signals to the capital market. The announcement of a new bank loan, the revision of an already existing loan, or the extension of a line-of-credit, signal the capital market that an independent monitoring of the firm's credit has resulted in a positive action by the bank.

CHAPTER FOUR

THE LAW OF INSIDER TRADING

The objective of this chapter is to provide a comprehensive analysis of insider trading laws. Given that laws are written in sufficiently general terms to allow the courts flexibility in interpretation, a comprehensive incorporation of the law and case precedents is required to provide the necessary link to the financial evaluation of insider trading.

Insider Trading Laws

The 1934 Act: Section 16

Before the passage of the Securities Exchange Act of 1934 there was virtually no regulation in the United States prohibiting insider trading. Cases against insider trading were decided on the basis of existing common law and were often unsuccessful. During this period, insider trading was generally treated as an acceptable perquisite granted to corporate insiders. For example, in *Goodwin v. Agassiz* (1933),[1] the plaintiff sold his shares after reading in a newspaper article that the company had discontinued its copper exploration in a certain area. Corporate directors knew, however, that the company was planning further exploration, and they were buying additional shares based on their nonpublic information. When the value of the firm's shares rose upon the release of the information, the plaintiff sued for damages. The Massachusetts Supreme Court denied recovery, arguing that the directors did not have a face-to-face transaction with the plaintiff because the transaction was conducted through the stock exchange.

The 1934 act, passed largely in response to securities abuses before the stock market crash, dealt explicitly with the issue of corporate insider trading. As noted previously, Section 12(b) of the act requires directors, officers, and large shareholders to register with the SEC and disclose

---

[1]Goodwin v. Agassiz, 283 Mass. 358, 186 N. E. 659 (1933).

their ownership in the firm. And Section 16(a) requires registered insiders to file statements with the SEC within ten days of the close of each calendar month of any changes in their holdings in the firm, while Section 16(b) makes short-swing profits recoverable by the firm. (A short-swing transaction involves a matching purchase and sale, or sale and purchase within a six month period.) Section 16(c) prohibits short selling by insiders in their own firms' shares.

However, the 1934 act contained loopholes that weakened its effectiveness as a deterrent to insider trading. For example, while the SEC has control over the content of the disclosure requirements under section 16(a), it has no power to force the disgorgement of the short swing profits. This leaves managers, directors, and shareholders to take legal actions for the disgorgement. The former, however, have little incentive to sue. Thus, the monitoring of such activities is effectively left to shareholders. Given that most shareholders hold small proportions of the outstanding shares, a free rider problem prevents shareholder actions. The principal incentive to the enforcement of this Section is left with attorneys to bring such suits. The precedent was set in the case of *Smolowe v. Delendo Corp.* (1943) in which the court granted fees for the plaintiff's attorneys. The result is a potentially effective enforcement process. A group of attorneys keeps track of 16(a) fillings, and whenever there is a match they find a small shareholder as their client and subsequently file suit on his or her behalf. The courts have refused to bar such actions as unethical, reasoning that Congress must have intended to accept the approach as the only means of enforcing this section of the law.

Section 16(b) is different from other anti-insider trading laws in that it does not require finding fraud, and its enforcement is in private hands. Furthermore, it is irrelevant whether the insider has access to material nonpublic information at the time of the transaction.

The scope of Section 16(b) is limited in three respects. First, it applies only to high-level executives who are required by Section 16(a) to file a form 3 with the SEC upon their designation as insiders and subsequent filings of form 4 within ten days after the end of each month in which a change in holdings occurs. Other insiders (or tippees) who may have access to material nonpublic information are not included. Second, the law requires the matching of two transactions (buy and sell or sell and buy) and does not involve only sales or only purchase transactions. Third, the matching transactions have to occur within a six-month period. These limitations have made Section 16(b) a less than effective tool against insider trading.

In 1991, the SEC made substantial revisions in the rules applied under Section 16. These changes occurred in response to developments in the trading of derivative securities, growth of diverse employee benefit plans, and increases in filing delinquencies.

The 1934 Act: Section 10(b)

One of the most widely used legal rules against insider trading to date has been the anti-fraud Rule 10b-5, which was adopted by the SEC in 1942:

> It shall be unlawful for any person, directly or indirectly, by the use of any means or instrumentality of interstate commerce, or of the mails, or of any facility of any national securities exchange, 1) to employ any device, scheme, or artifice to defraud, 2) to make any untrue statement of a material fact or to omit to state a material fact necessary in order to make the statements made, . . . or 3) to engage in any act, practice, or course of business which operates or would operate as fraud or deceit upon any person, in connection with the purchase or sale of any security (Ratner 1988, p. 130).

The SEC has a more active role in the enforcement of Rule 10b-5. It can take administrative actions against registered traders, such as brokers and dealers; ask the federal courts to force disgorgement of profits and impose penalties; and refer violators of Rule 10b-5 to the Department of Justice for criminal prosecution (Prentice 1987, pp. 628—629).

Rule 10b-5 was applied for the first time in the case of Cady, Roberts & Co. (1961).[2] Administrative proceedings were brought to determine whether leakage of the news of an impending dividend cut by a board member to a stockbroker and subsequent sale of securities by the broker violated the rule. The broker was subsequently suspended from the New York Stock Exchange for twenty days. The case established what is now known as the disclose or abstain rule. This rule requires

[2]40 SEC 907 (1961).

those who have access to material nonpublic information to either disclose it or abstain from trading based on that information. The disclose or abstain rule was later successfully applied in the case of the *SEC v. Texas Gulf Sulphur Co.*[3] in which the purchase of company stock by insiders prior to the announcement of a mineral discovery was ruled to have violated 10b-5. An insider's duty to disclose information or his duty to abstain from dealing in his company's securities arises only in "those situations which are essentially extraordinary in nature and which are reasonably certain to have a substantial effect on the market price of the security if disclosed."[4]

More recently, the Supreme Court has ruled on three occasions on the scope of Rule 10b-5. First, in 1980, it ruled in the case of *Chiarella v. United States*.[5] The case involved a printer, Vincent Chiarella, who as a markup-man in a printing firm, had identified the concealed names of several tender offer targets from documents submitted for printing. He subsequently traded in the target firms' shares and netted profits totalling $30,000. The SEC discovered the transactions and asked the Department of Justice to bring criminal charges against Chiarella for the violation of Rule 10b-5. The trial court convicted him and the Second Circuit Court affirmed the conviction. In an appeal to the U.S. Supreme Court, however, the conviction was overturned. The Court argued that the duty to disclose or abstain is only applicable when there is fiduciary duty involved.

The Supreme Court's Chiarella rule prompted the SEC to adopt Rule 14e-3 (1980) explicitly prohibiting trading by any person (inside or outside the firm) with access to material nonpublic information about impending tender offers. Since Rule 14e-3 is based on statutory authority independent of Section 10(b), the limitations imposed by the requirement to establish a breach of fiduciary duty under Rule 10b-5 (e.g., Chiarella) do not apply. This provides a broader scope to the applicability of Rule 14e-3 than it does to Rule 10b-5. A case in point

---

[3]401 F. 2d 833 (2d Cir. 1968).

[4]Supra note 3.

[5]445 U.S. 222 (1980).

is *United States v. Chestman*[6] in which the Second Circuit's en banc decision upheld the validity of Rule 14e-3 while imposing new limits on Rule 10b-5. The Court ruled that trading based on material nonpublic information does not necessarily violate Rule 10b-5 unless the trader has explicitly agreed to keep the information confidential, has misappropriated the information, or has a fiduciary duty to disclose or abstain. This decision strengthened Rule 14e-3 in the tender offer cases and limited the coverage of Rule 10b-5 in instances not involving information about a pending tender offer.

In 1983, the Supreme Court ruled in *Dirks v. SEC*[7] by referring to its decision in the Chiarella case. The case involved a financial analyst who discovered massive fraud involving the Equity Funding Corporation, a large insurance firm. He attempted to disclose the information by contacting *The Wall Street Journal*, which chose to ignore it. Subsequently, he instructed his clients to sell their shares in the firm. Shortly thereafter, California insurance authorities discovered the fraud and its disclosure lowered the share price from $26 to $15. The SEC censured Dirks for violating Rule 10b-5 and the District of Columbia Court of Appeals ruled against him. Upon his appeal to the Supreme Court, the Court emphasized its decision in the Chiarella case and ruled that the defendant did not have any fiduciary duty to the firm's stockholders and, therefore, had no obligation to either disclose the information or abstain from trading.

Under certain circumstances, however, a person who receives material nonpublic information (tippee) from an insider (tipper) may be required to disclose or abstain liability under Rule 10b-5. The tippee is responsible to disclose or abstain if the following conditions hold: 1) the insider tips the material nonpublic information for personal gains, hence, breaching fiduciary duty of loyalty; and 2) the tippee knows that by tipping, the insider has breached the duty of loyalty (Langevoort 1992). If both conditions hold, the tipper and tippee are liable. The first condition is broadly defined to include not only the pecuniary benefits but also gains received through enhancements in reputation, or what comes from providing favors to friends and acquaintances.

---

[6]947 f.2d 551 (2d Cir. 1991)(en banc).

[7]463 U.S. 646 (1983), footnote 14.

While the Chiarella and Dirk decisions restricted the SEC's enforcement power by narrowing the coverage of anti-insider trading rules, a third case involving a *Wall Street Journal* reporter passed the rigid interpretation of the Supreme Court and popularized what is now known as the misappropriation theory. The theory holds that anyone who trades on information entrusted to them for personal gains in breach of fiduciary duty is in violation of the anti-fraud provision of Rule 10b-5. In contrast to the disclose or abstain rule in which fraud is committed through failure to disclose information to other market participants, the misappropriation theory applies to cases in which the fraud is on the parties who entrusted the information to the fiduciary. The following example is an application of the theory. R. Foster Winans, the co-author of the "Heard on the Street" column had leaked advance information of the names of the companies to be mentioned in forthcoming articles to a Kidder, Peabody broker, Peter Brant.[8] In a series of transactions based on the information, the broker netted $690,000, of which $31,000 was paid to Winans. The government alleged that the reporter had misappropriated information that was the property of the *Journal* for personal profit. The misappropriation theory, first applied in 1982, had neither been legislated by Congress nor affirmed by the Supreme Court.[9] The Court ruled 8 to 0 in favor of mail and wire fraud convictions but 4 to 4 on the securities fraud issue. Nonetheless, the tie was sufficient to affirm the earlier conviction. The Court indicated that "the object of the scheme was to take the *Journal's* confidential business information, the publication schedule and contents of the Heard column and its intangible nature does not make it any less 'property' protected by the mail and wire fraud status." It was further argued that the "*Journal* has been deprived of its right to exclusive use of the information, for exclusivity is an important aspect of confidential business information and most private property, for that matter." The fact that the Court did not overturn the misappropriation theory, even when it included a reporter, provided government prosecutors with a powerful new weapon with which to indict stockbrokers, arbitragers, and other employees of

---

[8]United States v. Carpenter, 108 S. Ct. 316 (1987).

[9]Prior examples of the application of the misappropriation theory include United States v. Newman, 664 F.2d 12 (2d Cir. 1981); SEC v. Materia, 745 F. 2d 197 (2d Cir. 1984).

the investment banking community on the basis that misappropriation of information constitutes fraud.

Despite the successful prosecution of the Winans case, the SEC was frustrated by the ineffectiveness of the enforcement activities of existing anti-insider trading rules. Up to this point the SEC had two remedies available to it in its enforcement efforts. It could seek an injunction against future violations of the regulation, and it could force disgorgement of the profits made or losses avoided in an insider trading transaction. Successful enforcement of the rules by the SEC would bring defendants to their previous financial position. In the view of the SEC, therefore, one could not lose from insider trading. Furthermore, up to this point there was no statutory authority in the securities laws for the SEC to penalize insider trading other than asking the Department of Justice for a criminal prosecution. A criminal prosecution of the insider trading provisions of the securities laws, however, requires all the safeguards provided for the defendant including the right for a jury trial, and proof of guilt beyond a reasonable doubt. Moreover, the decision to prosecute is ultimately made by the Department of Justice and not by the SEC, which adds another layer of uncertainty to the process and slows down enforcement efforts. A combination of these factors may explain why criminal prosecutions of insider trading in the five decades following the passage of the 1934 act were so rare.

The Insider Trading Sanctions Act of 1984

Dissatisfaction with the effectiveness of enforcement procedures in deterring insider trading prompted the SEC to lobby Congress to pass the Insider Trading Sanctions Act of 1984 (ITSA).[10] ITSA provided a powerful weapon to the SEC through its provision that allows the Commission to impose treble damages sanctions against anyone found to have tipped or traded based on material nonpublic information. The authorization of a civil penalty is a major shift in the approach taken by Congress in its handling of securities law violations and insider trading. Prior to the passage of ITSA, the only way to penalize illegal insider trading was through criminal prosecutions. It was only after a criminal conviction that a civil penalty could be imposed. In contrast to the stringent requirements of criminal prosecutions that demand guilt beyond

---

[10]Public Law 98-376 (98 Congress, 1984).

reasonable doubt, the civil enforcement requires only a preponderance of the evidence as the standard of proof. Under ITSA, therefore, the SEC is the plaintiff, not the Department of Justice, and the defendant is entitled only to procedural protection rather than all the constitutional safeguards provided to the defendant under criminal prosecutions.

The legislation applies to those that have violated any provisions of this title as well as those who have violated the anti-fraud provisions of the Securities Exchange Act. Furthermore, ITSA applies only to trading in the secondary market through national security exchanges or through broker-dealers. Purchase or sale of securities in the primary market and those conducted face-to-face are excluded from the coverage of this title.

To measure the profits made, the court must calculate the difference between the price paid and the trading price within a reasonable period after the public dissemination of information. The court, therefore, will ignore the sale price if it is conducted long after public dissemination of the information. For example, if the purchase price is ten dollars and it increases by five dollars upon the public announcement of information but the trader decides to sell it a year later at a price of twenty, the profit made is still five dollars. Conversely, if a year later the price has fallen to its original level of ten dollars, the trader still is assumed to have profited five dollars. What constitutes reasonable time to allow for full dissemination of information is determined in the context of case law and can vary from shortly after the public announcement to a much longer period depending on the nature of the information. At the extreme, if it is believed that dissemination will be gradual, it is possible that the court will use the sale price to determine the profit. Upon determining the profit, the SEC may ask for disgorgement of the profit and treble damages amounting to a quadruple profits sanction.

There are remaining problems, however. Chief among them is the lack of a clearly defined notion of illegal insider trading. Civil prosecutions are conducted in the previous framework of illegal insider trading definitions provided in the case law under sections 10(b) and 14(e). These definitions are vague, and the case law is far from uniform in its interpretation.

The Insider Trading and Securities Fraud Enforcement Act of 1988

The SEC sought further sought to restrict insider trading by asking Congress to pass more legislation. Congress passed the Insider Trading and Securities Fraud Enforcement Act (1988 act)[11] on November 19, 1988. The 1988 act provided for bounties to informers of up to ten percent of insider trading profits and increased the maximum jail term to ten years. Perhaps the most striking aspect of this act is its requirement that public corporations adopt explicit policies to police employee insider trading. The act created a strong economic incentive for such action "through the broadening of controlling person civil penalty liability to supervise vigorously their employees." (The controlling person includes employers, managers, or those with power to influence or control the activities of another person.) The 1988 act gives the SEC the authority to impose penalties against controlling persons of up to $1 million, or three times the profits realized or losses avoided by insider traders, whichever is greater, if the SEC can establish that such persons knowingly or recklessly failed to take appropriate actions to prevent the violation before it occurred. (For a survey of corporate compliance programs see Weinberger 1990).

Theories of Insider Trading Liability and Governmental Enforcement

In this section we focus on the main theories of liability that the government uses in its enforcement of the law. What is striking here is that some of the early provisions of the law (e.g., Section 16(b)) seem to be less effective in the campaign against insider trading than other laws that were not explicitly written to deter insider trading (e.g., RICO).

Section 16(b) is very narrow in scope. It provides for shareholders to take legal action against registered insiders who have gained short swing profits. This action may lead to the disgorgement of the profits to the corporation. The scope is narrow because the law requires matching transactions within a six month period. If only one transaction takes place, even if it is quite profitable, no course of action is taken under this title. Or if the matching transactions take place within a period greater than six months, there is no liability. Finally, short swing profits do not have to be made based on material nonpublic information; rather, any short swing profit is recoverable. There is one exception to 16(b)'s ineffectiveness, however. The court allows attorneys to keep track of 16(a) filings and, as noted earlier, to file suit on behalf of a

---

[11]Public Law No. 100-704, 102 Stat. 4677 (Nov. 19, 1988).

small shareholder. The court has granted fees for the plaintiff's attorneys. A review of insider trading cases of the past two decades, however, suggests that government enforcement is often based on laws other than 16(b).

We next focus on the rules that serve as the government's principal weapons against insider trading. These include the abstain or disclose rule under Rule 10b-5, the misappropriation theory that was developed in the Winans case, Rule 14e-3 applied in the tender offer cases, and RICO, which has been used effectively in recent years despite the fact that it was not originally intended for its current use.

The Abstain or Disclose Theory Under Rule 10b-5

The abstain or disclose theory was first initiated in 1961 in *Cady Roberts & Co*[12] and was subsequently applied in *SEC v. Texas Gulf Sulphur Co.*[13] It stated that anyone who is in possession of material nonpublic information should either disclose it to the investing public before to trading or abstain from trading. The Supreme Court's landmark rule in 1980 in *Chiarella v. United States*[14] helped to clarify and limit the scope of the disclose and abstain rule. This ruling required that to impose the disclose or abstain rule, the trader must be a fiduciary to the firm and consequently to its shareholders. Absent the duty, the trader has no liability.

The reversal of Chiarella's conviction limited the application of the disclose or abstain theory to only registered insiders. The question was raised as to the liability of the tippee if the tip is received from an individual who is a fiduciary. The issue was further clarified in *Dirks v. SEC*[15] in which the Supreme Court established that in order to impose liability on the tippee, the tipper must be a fiduciary and the tip has to result in personal profit for the tipper. Absent personal gains in the Dirks case, the court reversed the early ruling. Subsequently the

---

[12]Supra note 2.

[13]Supra note 3.

[14]Supra note 5.

[15]463 U.S. 646 (1983).

definition of personal gains was broadened to include not only explicit personal financial gains but also subjective gains such as gains to one's reputation, and gaining a "warm glow" from providing information to a friend. A tippee's liability, therefore, is derived from whether or not a tipper breaches fiduciary duty for personal gains.

The Supreme Court ruling in the Dirks case was not all bad news for the SEC, since it also broadened the definition of an insider. The court ruled that while a person may not fit the definition of a registered insider, that person may still be privy to material nonpublic information due to temporary positions such as serving the firm in the capacity of an outside attorney, accountant, or investment advisor. Temporary insiders are subject to the disclose or abstain rule. The disclose or abstain rule remains as one of the most effective tools in the enforcement of the insider trading law.

The Misappropriation Theory

Unlike in the disclose or abstain rule, the misappropriation theory involves parties outside the firm. The theory was developed in *United States v. Carpenter*[16] in which R. Foster Winans, a coauthor for the Heard on the Street column in *the Wall Street Journal* had disclosed the content of his forthcoming articles to a broker who traded based on that information and provided a kickback to Winans. The information involved did not come from an insider to the firm. It was information that Winans himself had produced. But since he was an employee of *the Wall Street Journal,* the information he had produced was the property of *the Journal*. Therefore, by using the information for his personal gain he violated his fiduciary duty toward his employer.

Rule 14e-3: Tender Offer Information

While both the disclose or abstain theory and the misappropriation theory involve breach of fiduciary duty, rule 14e-3 does not require such a condition. In 1980, the SEC adopted this rule in response to limitations set by the Supreme Court in the Chiarella case that required a fiduciary duty to impose liability on the trader. Rule 14e-3 states that if a trader knows or has reason to know the information received is from

---

[16]Supra note 8.

an insider, or a tender offer, the trader has a duty to disclose or abstain from trading regardless of fiduciary duty. The Second Circuit's en banc decision in *United States v. Chestman*[17] in 1991 confirmed the effectiveness of this theory.

Mail and Wire Fraud

If the disclose or abstain rule, the misappropriation theory, and Rule 14e-3 do not bring a successful prosecution of an insider trading case, prosecutors may apply the mail and wire fraud statutes. The mail and fraud statutes proscribe devices or schemes to gain money or property by means of false or fraudulent pretenses or promises through the use of mail or interstate phone facilities. A striking example of the effectiveness of the mail and wire statutes is the case of Carpenter, in which the court was split 4-4 in the misappropriation argument but upheld the conviction unanimously under the mail and wire fraud charges.

Other Laws Used in Enforcement: The Case of RICO

In addition to the existing anti-insider trading laws, prosecutors have sought to use other laws to deter insider trading. One such example is the application of the Racketeer Influenced and Corrupt Organization (RICO) Act. Passed in 1970, RICO was to be used against criminal infiltration of legitimate businesses and labor unions by organized crime. In recent years, however, civil filings under RICO have increased substantially. Of nearly one thousand cases filed during 1988, more than 90 percent were against legitimate businesses and individuals who were not involved in organized crime.[18] Supreme Court Justice William Rehnquist has summarized the emerging consensus:

> Virtually everyone who has addressed the question agreed that civil RICO is now being used in ways that Congress never intended when it enacted the statute in 1970. Most of the civil suits filed under the statute have nothing to do with organized

---

[17]Supra note 6.

[18]"Second Thoughts on RICO," *The Wall Street Journal,* May 19, 1989, p. A10.

> crime. They are garden variety civil fraud cases of the type traditionally litigated in state courts. Why does the statute work this way? In part, because it creates a civil counterpart for criminal wire fraud and mail fraud prosecutions. It does this by stating that acts indictable under those provisions, as well as many other types of criminal acts, are capable of establishing the "pattern of racketeering" that is the predicate for a civil RICO action.[19]

The criminal "predicate acts" that give rise to civil suits include robbery, murder, and securities fraud, and the use of the telephone or the mail for illegal purposes. Since almost all securities transactions involve the mail or telephones, they can be alleged to be fraudulent acts under RICO.

The first RICO charges involving securities law violations occurred in 1987 when Rudolph Giuliani, then a U.S. Attorney in New York, dispatched fifty federal marshals equipped with weapons and bulletproof vests to raid Princeton/Newport's offices near the Princeton University Campus. Subsequently, the firm and its five partners were indicted on charges of being involved in a racketeering criminal enterprise based on alleged tax fraud using bogus stock deals.

The severity of the conditions imposed under RICO may have contributed to the notoriety of some cases. Those indicted under RICO must post a significant portion of their assets as security that the government will be entitled to if it wins a conviction. The size of the bond and the time between the indictment and trial may be long enough to pose great uncertainty for a business. In the case of Princeton/Newport, the prosecutors demanded pretrial forfeitures of tens of millions of dollars. This lead investors such as the Harvard endowment to withdraw its money, forcing Princeton/Newport into pretrial liquidation. It was a similar threat of RICO that forced Drexel Burnham Lambert to plead guilty to other nonracketeering charges including six criminal counts of mail, wire, and securities fraud and to agree to pay $650 million in fines.

Perhaps the most significant securities-related RICO case to date is that brought against Michael Milken, formerly of Drexel Burnham Lambert. The 98-count indictment from a federal grand jury provided

---

[19]William Rehnquist, "Get RICO Cases Out of My Courtroom," *The Wall Street Journal,* May 19, 1989, p. A10.

the government with a claim on over $1.2 billion of Milken's assets. This forced Milken to plead guilty to technical offenses rather than enduring a RICO trial.

In response to criticism of the way in which RICO has been used by prosecutors, there have been several actions by the three branches of government to reform RICO. For example, in July 1991 all RICO charges against Princeton/Newport partners, including tax and conspiracy charges, were dropped (*the Wall Street Journal,* January 15, 1992, P. A13). (Ironically, the Internal Revenue Service concluded that the firm had actually overpaid its taxes during the disputed period.) The fact, however, remains that the firm itself was forced into liquidation due to the consequences of the RICO indictment. This is the type of concern that is reflected in the William Rehnquist's final remarks regarding RICO:

> "I think that the time has arrived for Congress to enact amendments to civil RICO to limit its scope to the sort of wrongs that are connected to organized crime, or have some other reason for being in federal court."[20]

Summary

The current state of insider trading regulation can be summarized in the following manner. First, trading by registered insiders of the kind specified in Section 16 of the Securities Exchange Act of 1934 (short swing transactions) is expressly forbidden. Since the information on registered insider trading is publicly available, it is reasonable to assume that this type of illegal insider trading can be successfully deterred by the current structure of regulation. Second, an outsider who misappropriates inside information is also liable. Third, temporary insiders are prohibited from trading based on material nonpublic information. [21]

---

[20]Supra note 19.

[21]There is a large body of work in the legal literature that examines regulatory issues related to insider trading. See for example Brodsky and Swanson (1988), Brudney (1979), Carlton and Fischel (1983), Carney (1987), Cox (1986), Dooley (1980), Easterbrook (1981), Easterbrook and Fischel (1991), Garten (1987), Haddock and Macey (1987), Haft (1982), Heller (1982), Janvey (1986, 1987), Karjala (1982), Silver (1985), and Scott (1980).

In the next chapter we review the extant empirical evidence on insider trading, which supports the contention that it is a pervasive and ubiquitous phenomenon.

CHAPTER FIVE

THE EMPIRICAL LITERATURE ON INSIDER TRADING: AN OVERVIEW

The contemporaneous development of rigorous theories of asset pricing and market efficiency in the mid-1960s led naturally to recognition of the need for a closer examination of the role of information generally and private information specifically in the workings of capital markets. The trickle of empirical research on insider trading in the early part of that decade has been supplanted by a steady stream of research addressing numerous issues, including the implications of asymmetric information, actions of insiders around various firm-related events, and the effects of regulation on the actions of those with private information. In this chapter, we focus on the extant empirical research on insider trading in finance. To facilitate an orderly examination of a large body of material, the following discussion is divided into four (nonmutually exclusive) sections:

1. The Nature and Characteristics of Insiders' Transactions
2. Insider Trading and Information Efficiency
3. Insider Trading and Managerial Decisions
4. Insider Trading and the Efficacy of Regulation

The first category is largely descriptive and consists primarily (but not entirely) of work done up to the mid-1960s. Although some of these early studies are somewhat hampered by the lack of a machine-readable database, an overall reading of this portion of the literature suggests that insiders were generally able and willing to utilize their monopolistic access to information to earn abnormal returns. The seminal work of Pratt and DeVere (1978) and Lorie and Niederhoffer (1968) provides compelling evidence that insiders' transactions have informational content. From this point, the empirical research follows a rather logical progression in examining the implications that insiders both possessed and acted upon information not possessed by other capital market participants.

The second category of literature examines insiders' transactions in the context of the efficient markets hypothesis (EMH). Rapid theoretical and methodological advances facilitated more numerous (and perhaps more reliable) computations of the returns earned by insiders on their own transactions. That insiders have historically earned excess returns is now taken as a given by most researchers in the area, and it is generally (although by no means universally) accepted that the strong form of the EMH does not hold.

A related question is whether or not the semistrong form of the EMH also holds in this context; i.e., can outsiders expect to earn abnormal returns by mimicking the reported transactions of insiders? It is natural for rational investors to ask whether or not the actions of insiders constitute viable signals with which they (i.e., outsiders) can improve their investment results. The results are somewhat mixed. However, it is probably safe to say that early researchers concluded that aping insiders is a profitable strategy, while subsequent research suggests that abnormal returns to be earned are minimal at best, after accounting for transactions costs and bid-ask spreads, as well as risk and firm-size premia.

A third avenue of research concerns the transactions of registered insiders in the periods surrounding managerial decisions that are expected to affect firm value. Finding that insiders systematically act prior to managerial decisions in order to earn excess returns (or to avoid losses) suggests once again a willingness and ability to exploit nonpublic information. The type of information that is acted upon or, alternatively, the types of events that have been shown to be associated with insider trading, are the subject of this section.

Finally, given that some form of insider trading regulation has existed in America since the passage of the Securities Act of 1933, one must wonder how to reconcile evidence suggestive of the ability of insiders to earn excess returns by using private information with the existence of laws formulated to prohibit such activities. In this final section we examine the effects of regulation on insider transactions. The results of the empirical studies published to date suggest that until the 1980s, insider trading regulation was relatively ineffectual in terms of its deterrent capability. More recent evidence indicates, however, that, beginning in approximately 1984, registered insiders displayed reduced willingness to exploit their monopolistic access to information. From this research comes the even more interesting result that insider trading by firm managers may have been supplanted by insider trading by "outside-insiders" —- i.e., those who are neither employed by nor are large stockholders in the firm in whose shares trading occurs, but who have obtained nonpublic information by some other means. The chapter concludes with a summary of the evidence and provides suggestions for future research.

The Nature and Characteristics of Insider Trading

The Characteristics of Insider Transactions

One of the earliest examinations of insider trading is by Smith (1941), who documents insider transactions over the 1935—1939 period. Smith's pathbreaking study serves as a precursor to much of the empirical research that flowered two-and-one-half decades later, dealing with such issues as (a) the importance of the ratio of insider purchases to insider sales as an indicator of insider sentiment, (b) the effects of insider volume on market prices, and (c) the predictive ability of insider trading. His findings are largely descriptive, but generally suggest that insiders of the period were willing to exploit their monopolistic access to nonpublic information for personal gain, a result that appears repeatedly in subsequent work.

In another early study, Wu (1964) examines insider transactions in the shares of fifty randomly selected NYSE firms over the 1957—1961 period in order to determine (a) how actively insiders traded in their own firms' shares, (b) how profitable insiders' trades were, and (c) whether or not insiders' trades affected market prices. Although his data set is small and the empirical methodology is relatively primitive compared to that employed in later studies, Wu's results are undeniably of interest. First, he finds that nearly all of the registered insiders studied were net sellers of their own firms' shares over the sample period, which is consistent with virtually all of the subsequent research. Second, Wu finds that across insider groups, directors and owner-directors were the most active traders in the years studied, while large (nonmanager) shareholders were the least active traders. Third, Wu reports that insiders were "not active in the market even in times of sustained price movements" (p. 381). In other words, his results, unlike much subsequent research results, do not suggest the willingness to use nonpublic information.

The work of Lorie and Niederhoffer (1968) represents one of the earliest empirical studies of insider trading in the modern era (i.e., the period coincident with the development of modern financial theory).

They provide pioneering results in measuring and documenting both the characteristics and the predictive properties of insiders' transactions.[1]

Utilizing a random sample consisting of 105 NYSE firms in existence from January 1950 through December 1960, their key findings can be placed into two categories: descriptive statistics and the assessment of the information content of insiders' transactions. With respect to the former, their results indicate that (a) there is a high degree of variation in transaction sizes across insider groups, and (b) insiders tended to be net purchasers of their firms' shares in the sample period.[2]

With respect to the predictive properties of insiders' transactions, Lorie and Niederhoffer report that insider transactions within a firm display "a pervasive continuity" — i.e., purchases tend to be followed by purchases and sales by sales. They conclude, therefore, that a "change in direction of activity probably is of importance in deducing insiders' expectations concerning their stocks" (p. 45). Additionally, it is concluded that "[i]nsiders are superior forecasters of large [greater than 8 percent] changes" in the prices of their own firms' shares, and that intensive trading by insiders precedes periods of abnormal performance (using the DJIA as a benchmark).

Further evidence of the information content of insiders' transactions is provided in a contemporaneous[3] study by Pratt and DeVere (1978) of approximately 52,000 open-market purchases and sales by insiders in

---

[1]Lorie and Niederhoffer's study popularized the use of the "intensive trading month" as a signal of insider transactions. This measure was first employed by Rogoff (1964) to reduce noise in the measurement of insider transactions. An intensive trading month is defined as a calendar month in which, for a given firm, there are at least three buyers (sellers) and no sellers (buyers).

[2]The latter result is different from most of the other published research, but may be attributable to the fact that both option and rights exercise transactions are included as purchases by Lorie and Niederhoffer, while most other researchers exclude these transactions completely. At the current time, the question of whether option exercise is a bullish or bearish event remains an unresolved empirical question.

[3]Although performed at roughly the same time as the Lorie and Niederhoffer study, the Pratt and DeVere work was not published until it appeared in *Modern Developments in Investment Management*, edited by James Lorie and Richard Brealey in 1978.

NYSE firms between January 1960 and June 1966. The authors examine share price performance following buy and sell signals. They conclude that large returns would have been earned by those who bought at the same time as the insiders under examination. Even more surprising is their conclusion that buying shares as much as *two months* following a buy signal would have been profitable for one outside the firm.

The characteristics of insiders' transactions in nonlisted firms are examined by Lin and Howe (1990), who also employ similar signals to delineate periods of intensive insider buying or selling. Consideration of the transactions of insiders in OTC firms over the period from January 1975 through April 1983, leads them to conclude that

> 1. There is no evidence of seasonality in insider transactions either by month or year,
> 2. Larger firms are associated with a greater number of intensive trading months than smaller firms,
> 3. The firms in their sample display 1.2 times as many intensive selling months as intensive purchase months,
> 4. Intensive purchase firms are, on average, smaller than intensive selling firms,
> 5. Insiders consistently made the right own-wealth maximizing decisions — i.e., intensive selling months followed periods of positive abnormal returns, and intensive purchase months followed periods of negative abnormal returns.

The authors infer from the latter result that insiders "refrain[ed] from purchasing stock until after the release of unfavorable information and . . . from selling stock until after favorable information [was] released" (p. 1278).

Lin and Howe also consider the importance of bid-ask spreads in determining the magnitudes of the abnormal returns reported and conclude that insiders' trades may have predictive content, although the existence of high bid-ask spreads in the OTC market may eliminate much of the profit opportunity both for insiders and for noninsiders.

Finally, they report that cumulative abnormal returns in the period following intensive trading months are unrelated to firm size, but positively related both to the size of the bid-ask spread, and to the insider's access to information (as proxied by his position within the firm). They conclude that, while there is "no support here for the notion that insiders of smaller firms take advantage of greater informational asymmetry in their stock transactions" (p. 1283), there is evidence that those who face higher transactions costs will trade on more valuable information, and that different insider groups possess different information. Further evidence of the existence of this information hierarchy effect can be found in several studies, including Nunn, Madden, and Gombola (1983) and Eyssell (1990).

Insider Trading and Firm Characteristics

If insider transactions convey information, it is reasonable to wonder exactly *what* information is being conveyed. One approach to addressing this issue is to consider the relationship between firm financial characteristics and the types of transactions that are observed. Finnerty (1976b) examines the financial characteristics of 854 NYSE firms in which insiders transacted during 1971. He utilizes multiple discriminant analysis to determine the degree to which one could categorize the firms into insider buying groups and selling groups on the basis of financial characteristics. Finnerty reports that the firms in which insiders were net buyers tended to be smaller, have higher earnings, and to pay larger dividends than those in which insiders were net sellers.

One of the most widely cited studies to date is that of Seyhun (1986), who examines 769 NYSE- and AMEX-listed firms for which at least one insider transaction was recorded between 1975 and 1981. These firms are stratified into five size groups with equity market values ranging from less than $25 million to greater than $1 billion. Both in terms of number of transactions and in dollar value, the bulk of the insider-trading activity consists of transactions by insiders of the firms in the two largest size categories. Interestingly, he reports that (a) insiders in the smaller firms tended to be net purchasers of their firms' shares, while insiders in the largest firms tended to be net sellers, and, (b) that insiders in small firms earned substantially greater abnormal returns than insiders in large firms (p. 201).

In sum, the abovementioned studies led the way for future researchers both by documenting some of the empirical regularities observed in insider transactions data collected by the Securities Exchange Commission, and by raising questions that continue to nag researchers to this day. Such issues as the magnitude of excess returns earned by insiders, as well as the ability of the rest of us to earn excess returns by mimicking insiders' actions are rooted in the early research. In the next section, we consider these and other questions more directly.

Insider Trading and Informational Efficiency

It is an axiom of capital market theory that those who have access to nonpublic information and the willingness to use it for trading purposes will be able to outperform those who do not. This is, of course, the essence of the "strong form" of the efficient markets hypothesis. The weak and the semistrong forms of the EMH focus, on the other hand, on the speed with which *publicly available* information is impounded in current market prices. If the market does not adjust immediately to the information conveyed in the trades of those with inside information, then others may be able to earn excess returns by investing on insiders' coattails, as it were.

As noted earlier, the results of the Pratt and DeVere (1978) study suggest that, even after a two-month lag, investors purchasing shares following a publicly available buy signal may earn large returns. This result has generated a great deal of interest for two reasons. First, it contradicts the semistrong form of the EMH, certainly a disturbing proposition for most students of modern finance. Second, from a practical standpoint, it suggests a relatively simple method for "beating the market" (i.e., for earning excess returns). In this section, we examine the empirical evidence related both to the ability of insiders themselves to earn excess returns, and to the ability of noninsiders to do likewise.

Insiders and Abnormal Returns

Perhaps the seminal paper on the profitability of insiders' transactions is that of Jaffe (1974b). In one of the first insider trading studies to employ modern event-study methodology,[4] Jaffe examines the profitability of transactions by officers, directors, and officer-directors in 200 large firms during five subperiods between 1962 and 1968. He reports that insiders tended to buy before abnormal share price increases and sell before abnormal share price decreases. Similar results for

---

[4]Pioneered by Fama, Fisher, Jensen, and Roll (1969), the event-study methodology allows the researcher to measure the average abnormal return on a portfolio of securities of firms which have been the subject of a specified event. By doing so, one measures the wealth effects of the event and, by inference, the expectations of market participants of its economic consequences. Brown and Warner (1980, 1985) describe and test some of the most common techniques used in event studies.

insiders in Canada and Great Britain are reported by Baesel and Stein (1979) and Pope, Morris, and Peel (1990), respectively.

Like Pratt and DeVere, Jaffe indicates that outsiders may be able to employ information from the public record of registered insiders' transactions (the SEC's *Official Summary*) to earn abnormal returns even after correcting for risk differentials and for transactions costs. He concludes "that investors can profit by prompt use of the *Official Summary's* information on intensive trading companies" (p. 427). But what is the source of the information used by insiders in earning abnormal returns? A crucial question not addressed directly by the early research is whether the nature of the information possessed by insiders is primarily unsystematic (i.e., firm-related) or systematic (i.e., related to the macroeconomy). Seyhun examines the magnitudes of the relationships between aggregate insider transactions and expected market returns, as well as the extent to which insiders were able to anticipate the stock market crash of 1987. The evidence provided by Seyhun indicates that while on the one hand, insiders have some capability to predict short-term market returns, they are better able to forecast the returns on the stocks of their own firms.

This ability varies with firm size, however. Seyhun indicates that insiders in smaller firms tend to trade on firm-specific information, while those in larger firms "who are less successful predictors of their own firms' performance" appear to trade more on the basis of macroeconomic factors.

On the other hand, Seyhun (1990b) contends that an examination of aggregate insider transactions indicates that the crash of 1987 was largely unanticipated. He states: "the absence of [insider] selling prior to October 19 suggests that the corporate insiders did not expect the imminent crash as late [as] October 16, 1987" (p. 1376). Consistent with the contention that insiders are better able than others to identify misvaluation situations in their own firms' shares, he reports that insiders reacted to the large and sudden drop in values by buying their firms' shares in record volumes in subsequent months. That is, registered insiders recognized that the drop in prices took market prices below their fundamental values and viewed the event as a buying opportunity. Further evidence consistent with this explanation can be found in Netter and Mitchell (1989).

Insider Transactions as an Investment Tool

We have already noted that several studies suggest that insiders' transactions are not, in every case, impounded immediately in market prices, even though they become public information upon publication in the *Official Summary*, as well as in newspaper columns (e.g., *The Wall Street Journal*'s "Inside Track") and in various investment newsletters. An early attempt to probe this matter more closely is found in Kerr (1980). Employing Lorie and Niederhoffer's unanimity principle as a means of sample selection, he finds few statistically significant differences in the monthly geometric mean returns of insider portfolios and the S&P 500 Index. He concludes that his results "suggest that knowledgeable investors have largely eliminated the inefficiency initial perceived by Pratt and DeVere and later by Jaffe . . . [n]on-insiders cannot use the information published in the Official Summary to earn excess economic profits" (p. 49). In a subsequent comment, however, Goldie and Ambachtsheer (1981) contend that, after correcting for methodological problems, Kerr's results instead "show that noninsiders *can* use the *Official Summary* to earn excess profits significantly more often than not" (italics in original).

A secular decline in the information content of published insider transactions information is noted by Trivoli (1980), who combines insider transactions information and firm financial data to construct a screen with which to select those firms most likely to experience superior performance. Broadly speaking, two criteria are applied: (a) the intensity of insider trading (measured by the difference in the number of buyers and sellers in a given month, and (b) firm financial performance relative to its industry peers. Trading intensity is used as an initial sample selection method, while relative financial performance serves to confirm insiders' signals. Upon comparison of the performance of the screened stocks, Trivoli concludes that, in general, sell signals are a stronger determinant of profitability than buy signals, and that the use of both insider transactions and firm financial data in combination may enhance one's ability to select superior securities.

More recent work, however, casts doubt on the value of the *Official Summary* as a tool for investors. Rozeff and Zaman (1988) contend that while outsiders do appear to be able to earn abnormal returns by aping insiders' transactions, the returns are largely a reflection of the well-documented size and earnings-price effects. Brick, Statman, and Weaver (1989), on the other hand, report that the magnitude (and even the existence) of the apparent excess returns earned by outsiders who buy shares following insider purchases are extremely sensitive to the specification of the return-generating model used to delineate normal returns.

Regardless of whether or not information on insiders' actions is truly of value, the fact that investors are willing to purchase the services of newsletters and advisory services that collect and analyze insider data suggests that it is *perceived* to have economic value. The perceived information content of insider transactions information has led to the publication of a number of investment newsletters that report and analyze insiders' transactions in order to make buy and sell recommendations, as well as a regular column in *The Wall Street Journal*, and relatively frequent articles in both the financial and the nonfinancial press. A representative study of newsletter recommendations is that of Benesh and Pari (1987), who examine the possibility that a noninsider may find it possible to earn abnormal returns by following the recommendations of one of the more popular newsletters. Their evidence is best characterized as mixed. They find that while the stocks listed in the newsletter displayed positive abnormal returns in the months preceding the listing, there is only weak evidence of abnormal returns to noninsiders who buy shares in response to open market purchases by insiders.

Based on the evidence above, we arrive at the following conclusions: First, it would appear that, historically, registered insiders have been able to utilize private, firm-related information to earn excess returns, although they have been less successful in anticipating changes in macroeconomic conditions. Further, the evidence suggests that any nonpublic information impounded in insiders' transactions is reflected rapidly in share prices, making examination of the *Official Summary* either by investors or newsletter writers a chore of questionable value. We now narrow our focus to examine specific events around which insider trading may be observed.

Insider Trading and Managerial Decisions

In the empirical research cited above, the emphasis was on changes in share prices around periods of heavy insider purchases and sales. Given the apparent tendency for insiders to exploit micro economic, rather than macro economic information, we consider in this section a body of evidence that examines the patterns of abnormal returns and insider trading volume around events that are the result of decisions by firm management and which have the potential to significantly impact firm value. Included are such events as earnings announcements, the decision to acquire another firm, to implement accounting changes, to initiate cash dividend payments, to engage in sell-offs, bankruptcies, or liquidations, and to issue securities.

Earnings Announcements

A relatively large volume of research examines the relationship between earnings announcements and insider trading. One of the most thorough studies was performed by Penman, who states that "[a]nnual earnings forecasts are published voluntarily by management and have been shown to convey information which, on average, affects stock prices . . . [t]hus there is potential for insiders to earn abnormal returns by taking market positions prior to these announcements" (1982, p. 480). Examining 550 voluntary earnings announcements over the 1968—1973 period, he finds that registered insiders tended to (a) purchase (sell) their firms' shares in the period immediately preceding favorable (unfavorable) earnings announcements, and to (b) sell (purchase) shares shortly after favorable (unfavorable) announcements. He concludes that "[t]hese data do suggest that insider use their forecast information in trading and time their trades relative to the forecast date" (1982, p. 491). In a subsequent paper, Penman (1985) reports that the timing of insider transactions relative to voluntary earnings forecasts is, in and of itself, a valuable piece of information.

The relationship between firm-specific events and insider activity is also noted in a related study by Elliot, Morse, and Richardson (1984), who examine insider transactions around several events, including annual earnings announcements that reflect large, unexpected earnings changes. Examining insiders' transactions in listed firms over the 1975—1979 period, Elliot, et al. find the strongest evidence of information-related trading to occur around *unexpected* earnings changes, particularly for small firms.

In his examination of the effectiveness of anti-insider trading regulation, Seyhun (1992) obtains somewhat different results. He examines changes in the nature of insider transactions during the 1980s. Among the events considered are insider transactions around quarterly earnings announcements. Computing a simple measure of unexpected earnings based on those of the previous four quarters, he defines timely (i.e., information-based) insider trading as that for which the net number of insider purchases is of the same sign as unexpected earnings change. Seyhun's results suggest that the tendency for insiders to trade prior to earnings announcements was marginal at the beginning of the period studied, and decreased with the imposition of increasingly severe penalties over time.

Takeover Bids

That regular earnings announcements were not strongly associated with abnormal insider trading is perhaps not surprising if one considers that earnings announcements represent events whose time of occurrence is known with a high degree of certainty, and whose content is widely anticipated (at least for large firms) by large numbers of analysts, market pundits, and investors. The onset of a takeover bid, on the other hand, is subject to much less market anticipation and generally has the potential to move stock prices much more dramatically. In this section we consider the existence of insider trading in the shares of both the bidder and the target firms in various types of control-related events.

One of the earliest attempts to link insider trading and takeover-related activities is found in Keown and Pinkerton (1981). They examine the market model residuals for a sample of 194 listed and nonlisted firms immediately before and after the announcement of a takeover bid. They find a pattern of significant positive abnormal returns beginning approximately one month prior to the announcement, and accelerating in the last five to eleven days. Further, total trading volume in the sample firms' shares is shown to increase dramatically over the same period. The authors conclude that "[t]he findings show what appears to be common knowledge on the street: impending merger announcements are poorly held secrets, and trading on this nonpublic information abounds" (p. 866).

Similar results are reported by Keown, et al. (1985), who also find that there is no significant difference in the magnitudes of the price run-ups between targets in which insiders were ultimately prosecuted for their actions, and targets in which there were no prosecutions.

The direct effect of insider trading on share prices is examined by Meulbroek (1992), who considers the price effects on 186 NYSE, AMEX, and OTC securities that were traded by those charged with insider activity by the SEC over the 1980—1989 period. The majority (79 percent) of the cases studied by Meulbroek involve insider trading related to an impending corporate control transaction.

Obtaining data on insider transactions from both public and nonpublic documents at the SEC, Meulbroek regresses observed returns on several variables measuring the announcement of public information, existence of insider trading, and contemporaneous news items about the firms in her sample. She comes to the following conclusions. First, average abnormal returns exceeding three percent occurred on days in which insiders traded, and nearly half of the cumulative abnormal return observed occurred on insider trading days. Second, excess returns on insider trading days were significantly larger than those on days without insider trading. Third, in the periods preceding takeover announcements, "forty-three percent of the preannouncement price movement occurs [on] insider trading days, twenty-five percent occurs on news days, and thirty-two percent occurs on days without insider trading or news announcements" (p. 34). And, after "subtracting the shares traded by inside traders, the volume on insider trading days does not appear to be significantly different than the volume on surrounding days close to the announcement of the inside information" (p. 39). Meulbroek concludes that her results "provide a foundation for the argument that stock price run-ups before takeover announcements reflect widespread insider trading" (p. 43).

Seyhun (1990a) attempts to determine if managerial motives are revealed by insiders' trades in the shares of firms that acted as bidders for other firms in the period 1975—1986. He finds that insiders in bidder firms tended to trade heavily prior to the announcement of a takeover bid, and that there is a significant relationship between the nature of the insiders' trades and the effect of the acquisition announcement on firm value. Specifically, insiders in takeover bids that were associated with positive (negative) excess returns tended to be net purchasers (sellers) of their firms' shares in the months leading up to the announcement. The results are, of course, completely consistent with the hypothesis that insiders utilized their access to nonpublic information to maximize their own wealth.

Interestingly, Seyhun's results also provide some evidence in support of the method-of-payment hypothesis, which suggests that the form of financing employed in a merger provides a signal to the market regarding managerial expectations on the bidder firms' prospects. According to this hypothesis, cash offers are interpreted by the market as indicative of undisclosed good news about the bidding firm and, and are therefore associated with positive abnormal returns around the announcement of the impending acquisition. Equity exchange offers, on the other hand, are viewed negatively by market participants. Seyhun finds that "top managers in bidder firms that offer some or all cash to the target firm are generally more optimistic than top managers in control firms", while for the equity-offering firms top managers "do not expect the takeover attempts (and the information released thereby) to reduce the stock prices of their firms" (p. 454).

Takeover bids of various types are often preceded by "toehold acquisitions"; i.e., sequential purchases of the target firm's shares by the ultimate bidder in order to gain leverage for the impending bid. The Williams Act requires that share purchasers make their positions known via the filing of form 13d with the Securities and Exchange Commission once their holdings surpass five percent of the outstanding shares, with further filings required as holdings increase in two percent increments. Holderness and Sheehan (1985) and Eyssell (1989) report share price increases preceding the initial 13D filing, consistent with either insider trading or the leakage of information about the impending filing (or both). In the latter study, it is reported that 1) registered insiders generally were heavy net purchasers prior to 13D filings, and 2) high-information insiders (i.e., those with the greatest access to nonpublic information) were much heavier purchasers than low-information insiders.

Accounting Changes

A large body of academic literature of accounting seeks to measure the economic consequences of accounting changes in order to determine the potential wealth or information effects that may be engendered in such changes. While most of this research has employed capital market reactions to the announcements of such changes as a measure of economic consequence, a few authors have focused on the actions of registered insiders. The logic, of course, is that, accounting changes that affect value are more likely to be associated with insider transactions than those that are not.

Larcker, Reder, and Simon (1983) examine insiders' transactions in a sample of firms expected to be affected by FASB Statement No. 19, which requires the adoption of the "successful-efforts" method of accounting for exploratory oil and gas drilling (as opposed to the full-cost approach also in use at the time). The authors find that, consistent with the proposition that insiders will act to maximize their own wealth, insiders in those firms expected to be adversely affected by the accounting change were net sellers in the period preceding the pronouncement. The conclusions of Larcker, et al. are supported in a subsequent study by King and O'Keefe (1986).

A similar approach is taken by Odaiyappa and Nainar (1992) in examining the valuation consequences of SFAS No. 33, which concerns the release of inflation-adjusted information. They hypothesize that one should observe an abnormal volume of sales by insiders in firms whose reported net income was reduced as a result of the mandated accounting change. It is concluded that, for the period studied (1975—1981), there was a significant positive relationship between earnings shrinkage and insider sales.

Dividend Initiation Announcements

John and Lang (1991) address an issue that has plagued financial researchers for decades: Are dividend increases unambiguous "good news" events? Although many would answer in the affirmative, it can also be persuasively argued that the payment of higher dividends signals a lack of future investment opportunities. John and Lang construct and test a model in which the interaction of the two signals - insiders' transactions and dividend announcements - constitute an efficient signalling equilibrium. They conclude that "[u]nexpected dividend increases, accompanied by unusual insider buying, signals good news and should elicit a positive stock price response. Dividend increases accompanied by unusual insider selling signal bad news and should elicit a *negative* stock price response." (italics in original.)

Firm Dissolution — Sell-Offs, Bankruptcies, and Voluntary Liquidations

Sell-Offs Hirschey and Zaima (1990) examine the informational content of bank debt and insider trading in the context of corporate sell-offs over the 1975—1982 period. They hypothesize that either or both of these variables reflects nonpublic information about the impending transaction. Essentially, it is their contention that, to the extent that a firm has been able to obtain bank financing, or that registered insiders have been net purchasers of their firms' shares, the sell-off will be viewed favorably by capital market participants. Their results indicate that both the presence of bank debt and net insider purchases are associated with more favorable reaction to sell-off announcements, consistent with their hypothesis. Using a similar data set and similar methodology, Hirschey and Zaima (1989) find that high levels of insider ownership and insider net purchases are associated with positive market reactions to sell-off announcements.

Bankruptcies and Voluntary Liquidations Gosnell, Keown, and Pinkerton (1992) contrast the transactions of insiders in OTC and listed firms that filed for bankruptcy in 1985—1987. Their results suggest that insiders of smaller, nonlisted firms were the heaviest net sellers prior to bankruptcy. Weaker results were obtained in tests of the transactions of those in listed firms, which may explain in part the differences in their results and those of Loderer and Sheehan (1989), who find little evidence to suggest excessive selling by insiders in NYSE and AMEX firms prior to bankruptcy.

Eyssell (1991), on the other hand, considers contrasts the transactions volumes of registered insiders in the months preceding bankruptcy and voluntary liquidation announcements, respectively, and finds that, while registered insiders in firms that ultimately filed for bankruptcy systematically reduced their shareholdings in the months preceding the announcement, insiders in firms which were ultimately liquidated were heavy net purchasers of their firms' shares prior to the price increase at the time of the announcement.

Security Issuance — IPOs and Seasoned Equity Offerings

Another firm event that affects share value is the issuance of new common stock. Myers and Majluf (1984) show that, in a market characterized by asymmetric information between managers and shareholders, selling new common stock is viewed as a signal of undisclosed adverse information. Karpoff and Lee (1991) examine seasoned equity offerings between 1975 and 1982 and find that, after adjusting for normal transaction patterns, corporate insiders sold significantly more shares than they purchased in the months preceding the offering announcement. That is, they avoided some of the losses imposed on other market participants. (As noted below, however, Eyssell and Reburn (1993) find that this pattern of behavior disappeared following the passage of the Insider Trading Sanctions Act of 1984.)

Initial public offerings (IPOs) provide yet another event with which to examine the actions of insiders for information content. Insider transactions following IPOs are examined by Eyssell and Kummer (forthcoming). Building on the signalling hypothesis of Leland and Pyle

(1977), the authors contend that one will observe 1) an inverse relationship between the initial returns and the proportion of the shares sold by insiders at the time of the offering, and 2) a positive relationship between the net sales by insiders in the post-offering period and the volume of shares sold by insiders at the time of the offering. Both of the hypothesized results are obtained, which leads the authors to conclude that insiders' transactions both at the time of and in the period following an IPO play a role in determining abnormal returns.

Insider Trading and the Efficacy of Regulation

The accumulated evidence on insider trading and managerial decisions is strongly suggestive of a world in which registered insiders believe themselves to be largely unencumbered by regulations designed to prevent them from trading on nonpublic information. This feeling of invincibility is made all the clearer when one takes into account the fact that most of the studies cited previously employed insider trading data *supplied to the regulatory authorities by the insiders themselves.* As a result, the accepted paradigm in finance has, at least until recently, held that insider trading regulation has been largely ineffectual.

The decade of the 1980s was, however, characterized by an explosion in the size and volume of corporate restructuring transactions — mergers, tender offers, LBOs, MBOs, MLPs; the list of methods employed to reconstitute the corporation is seemingly endless. Arshadi et al. (1992) argue that insider trading is a natural (and perhaps inevitable) by-product of an active market for corporate control. Highly valuable and largely unanticipated,[5] takeover-related information is created quickly and possessed by a relatively small number of people aware of its potential effect on share prices.

At the same time, however, the regulatory authorities instituted a policy of seeking out and prosecuting inside traders with a previously unheard-of zeal. Seyhun (1992) notes that from 1966 to 1980, the SEC prosecuted only 37 insider cases, an average of 2.6 cases per year. From

[5]While early evidence seemed to indicate the existence of accurate takeover prediction models based on publicly available financial information, Palepu (1986) notes that the existence of such models contradicts the semi-strong form of the EMH, and demonstrates that the previous research was methodologically flawed.

1982 to 1986, this figure rose nearly sevenfold. Keown, et al. (1985) state: "during the last four years alone the SEC has brought more than 40 cases against insider trading-**more than it had pursued in all its previous history**" (emphasis added — p. 329). However, the shift in regulatory attitudes toward insider trading is perhaps best exemplified by John Shad's widely quoted statement upon taking the position of SEC Chairman in 1981 that he would "come down on insider trading with hobnail boots."

Previously, we have examined empirical research detailing the occurrence of insider trading in the periods surrounding various managerial decisions. In this section we narrow our focus to concentrate on insider activity prior to takeover bids. We do so for a number of reasons. First, several researchers view the commonly observed preannouncement runups in the stock prices of takeover targets as *prima facie* evidence of trading by insiders. Others, as we will see, dispute the point. Second, insider trading prosecutions in the 1980s frequently involved those involved in takeover-related transactions, as exemplified by the string of prosecutions of (and the attendant publicity about) Dennis Levine, Ivan Boesky, Martin Siegel, and so many others. Finally, as a practical matter, it is with these circumstances that the data are most readily available. Below we consider the validity of the "runup as *prima facie* evidence" argument, then move to a discussion of the efficacy of insider trading regulation generally, and conclude with a question that remains unresolved at the present time: Just what does insider trading regulation accomplish?

Insider Trading and Price Runups — Evidence Pro and Con

Given the existence of both empirical and anecdotal evidence that seems to link takeover bids, preannouncement stock price runups, and insider trading, we focus on this *troika* in order to build a case for the persistence of insider trading. Anecdotal evidence linking the three events is provided by Seyhun, who notes that "80 percent of all insider trading cases brought by the SEC are associated with trading immediately before corporate takeovers or earnings announcements" (1992, p. 7).

More substantively, even a casual examination of the empirical mergers and acquisitions literature suggests that preannouncement price runups are common across takeover bid types and across time. Evidence of a runup in target firm share prices is apparent in much of the event-study work focusing on corporate control transactions. For example, the abnormal returns reported in the seminal work of Dodd and Ruback (1977), as well as studies by Asquith and Kim (1982), Dennis and McConnell (1986), and Eyssell and Arshadi (1993) all begin in advance of the takeover bid announcement date. And of course, we have previously cited studies by Keown and Pinkerton (1981) and Keown et al. (1985), which focus explicitly on pretakeover runups.

Not all researchers agree with the insider trading—based explanation of price runups, however. An alternative explanation is that the observed runup represents nothing more than the workings of an informationally efficient market; i.e., it is contended that investors seize upon every bit of publicly available information about the firm (including rumors) and are, on average, able to correctly anticipate its status as a future takeover target. Thus, the market anticipation hypothesis suggests that the role of insider trading in price runups is minimal, at best. This point of view is professed by Jensen and Ruback (1983), who contend that Keown and Pinkerton

> incorrectly conclude that 'impending merger announcements are poorly held secrets' and that the preannouncement price adjustments reflect insider trading and the leakage of inside information. They provide no tests of the plausible alternative hypothesis that the price adjustments prior to the 'announcement day' are unbiased responses to public information that increases the probability of a takeover . . . [i]nferences about insider trading or leakage require careful consideration of these issues. (footnote 6)

Thus, the source of preannouncement price runups becomes an empirical question. Two approaches have been taken to the construction of tests to answer this question. First, one might attempt to measure the extent to which information that could reasonably be interpreted to increase the possibility of a future takeover bid is made public prior to the official announcement of a takeover bid. Jarrell and Poulsen (1989a) examine price and volume changes in the shares of 172 firms that were takeover targets between 1981 and 1985. They also consider the effects of 1) form 13D filings, 2) takeover-related wire service stories, 3) foothold acquisitions by bidders, and 4) the relative friendliness of the takeover bid. After considering these factors, they conclude that approximately one-third of the observed price runups can be explained by the existence of public information sources, and state that "[t]he prospect of huge takeover premiums and the many kinds of clues legally available to skillful specialists assures us of an active market for information on prospective takeover targets."

On the other hand, Sanders and Zdanowicz (forthcoming) consider price and volume changes relative to an "initiation date" reported in proxy statements or tender offer bid (14D-1) filings, which indicates the first point at which the target firm is contacted by the bidder, and, of course, significantly precedes the first public announcement of the impending takeover bid. They find that share price runups begin virtually immediately upon the initiation of the takeover transaction. Given the high degree of secrecy associated with the initiation event, this seems to provide some credence for the insider-trading hypothesis relative to the market anticipation explanation.

A direct test of the importance of rumors is provided by Pound and Zeckhauser (1990), who examined all of the takeover rumors published in the *Wall Street Journal*'s Heard on the Street column over the period from January 1983 through December 1985. Implementing a trading rule in which investors purchase shares in the rumored takeover candidate on the rumor publication date and sell them at the sooner of the date of the formal bid announcement or the end of one year, the authors find that one would *not* have earned abnormal returns by acting on the publicly available information. Further evidence suggesting that price runups are observed prior to the publication of takeover-related information can be found in studies by Gupta and Misra (1988) and Haw, et al. (1990).

The second (and perhaps more powerful) approach is to document the existence of contemporaneous price runups and abnormal insider trading. One of the first published works to take this approach is Arshadi and Eyssell (1991), who examine a sample of firms that were tender offer targets over the 1976—1987 period. They subdivide the period into two regulatory eras corresponding to periods before and after the passage of the Insider Trading Sanctions Act of 1984. They report that for tender offers announced before the passage of the 1984 Act, dollar-volume-weighted preannouncement price runups averaged 9.89 percent *and* that registered insiders were heavy net purchasers of their own firms' shares. Meulbroek (1992) examines the transactions of insiders who have been prosecuted by the Securities and Exchange Commission, and reports that preannouncement price increases are significantly higher on days when insider trading occurred, and that "more stock price runup occurs on insider trading days than on either days with public news announcements or days without insider trading or news announcements."

We conclude that, while it is likely that a nontrivial portion of the price runups observed prior to takeover bids is attributable to market anticipation, the empirical evidence linking insider trading and price runups is quite strong. In documenting this relationship, however, a second phenomenon occurs: while the magnitude of the price increases remains large,[6] the volume of trading by registered insiders falls drastically.

The Effectiveness of Insider Trading Regulation

Discussion of the effectiveness of insider trading regulation tends to focus on the decade of the 1980s due largely to the confluence of three events during this period: 1) the wave of corporate restructuring, 2) the increase in regulatory zeal in prosecuting those suspected of trading on nonpublic information, and 3) the increased difficulty in separating those involved in structuring takeover deals from those speculating on their outcome (i.e., risk-arbitragers) .

Regulation and Insider Trading

The regulation of insider trading has generated countless pages debating both the pros and the cons of the issue. Fairness, economic efficiency, and the rewards to entrepreneurs are but a few of the arguments marshalled by proponents of one side or the other. In this section, however, we take the existence of regulation as a given, and focus instead on the efficacy of anti-insider trading regulation for its intended purpose, i.e., reducing (or eliminating) the practice of transacting on nonpublic information.

Perhaps the first modern study of the effects of regulation changes on insider trading is that of Jaffe (1974a), who tests the null hypothesis that increased regulation had no effect on the profitability of insiders' transactions. Jaffe computes excess returns for registered insiders in two groups of firms: 1) those employed by firms for which there are at least three more buyers (sellers) than sellers (buyers) in any month between April and October, 1961, and 2) those insiders in an analogous group of

---

[6]This statement should not be construed to mean that acquisition premia have remained constant over time. Jarrell and Poulsen (1989b), for example, document a decline in tender offer premiums from the 1970s to the 1980s.

firms with at least three more buyers (sellers) than sellers (buyers) in any month between December 1961 and November 1962. November 1961 marks a "regulatory line of demarcation" between (relatively) unregulated and regulated eras — i.e., before and after the famous Cady, Roberts decision. Jaffe finds that insiders in both groups earned large positive excess returns and that these returns are not significantly different from one another. Similar results are obtained for samples of abnormal returns computed before and after the indictments in the famous Texas Gulf Sulphur case, leading Jaffe to conclude that his results "do not suggest that regulation changes had an effect on the profitability of insider trading" (p. 109). Further, examinations of both monthly and daily transactions volume suggest that regulation changes had no effect on insider volume either. Given both the comprehensive nature of Jaffe's study, and the relative lack of regulatory action concerning insider trading, this view became the conventional wisdom among academic researchers for the next decade and a half.

Only recently has evidence appeared suggesting that the recent dramatic changes in both the scope and the nature of insider trading regulation have been effective in altering the behavior of some insiders. The motivation for much of this recent research is the dramatic increase in the vigor with which the regulatory authorities began to pursue inside traders beginning in the early 1980s. Major regulatory actions of the period include 1) the promulgation of Rule 14e-3, which was aimed specifically at those trading on information related to impending tender offer announcements; 2) the passage of the Insider Trading Sanctions Act of 1984; 3) the widely publicized prosecutions of Ivan Boesky, Dennis Levine, and others, beginning in May, 1986; 4) the 1988 passage of the Insider Trading and Securities Fraud Enforcement Act; and 5) the increasing use of RICO in the prosecution of inside traders.

In the previously mentioned work of Arshadi and Eyssell (1991), it is reported that, while target firm insiders were heavy purchasers of their firms' shares prior to tender offer announcements prior to the passage of the 1984 act, transactions patterns were reversed in the following period. They conclude that the passage of the Act served to deter registered insiders from trading prior to tender offers.

A broad analysis of the possible deterrent effects of both the passage of federal legislation and court cases in the 1980s is found in Seyhun (1992), who considers insiders' transactions from 1975 through 1989. Seyhun's sample contains the open-market purchase and sales transactions of registered insiders in NYSE, AMEX, and OTC firms, and the fifteen-year sample period is subdivided into three regulatory eras.

Seyhun performs two sets of tests — the first on the aggregate sample and the second on two subsamples: firms that have been takeover targets and firms that have reported earnings changes. For the aggregate sample, Seyhun reports that, as a proportion of outstanding shares, the volume of trading by insiders doubled from the first to the third period. Further, despite the increasingly restrictive regulatory environment, the profitability of insiders' transactions increased secularly. He concludes that insiders in the aggregate "appeared not to be concerned with changes in statutes, even on a temporary basis" (p. 16).

Narrowing his focus, Seyhun then explores the relative deterrent effects of statutory changes and case law by examining insider activity around specific events. His results indicate that insiders were increasingly reluctant to trade prior to earnings announcements, and that the trading activities of insiders generally and top executives specifically declined dramatically in the 30-day period preceding takeover bids, and did so in successive regulatory periods. Seyhun concludes that, while the enactment of federal statues (specifically ITSA and ITSFEA) do not appear to have a significant deterrent effect on insiders in the aggregate, "court cases regarding insider trading around earnings and takeover announcements did affect insider trading patterns."

Further evidence on the effects of federal legislation is provided by Eyssell and Reburn (1993), who perform a similar analysis on two samples of firms that issued seasoned equity: those that did so prior to the passage of the 1984 act, and those that did so after. Their results are consistent both with those of Karpoff and Lee (1992), who report heavier-than-usual insider sales prior to seasoned equity offering announcements (thus avoiding the concomitant price decreases), and with Arshadi and Eyssell (1991), in that the preponderance of registered insider sales activity prior to this event disappears following the passage of ITSA. That is, the 1984 act had a deterrent effect on registered insiders.[7]

The studies cited above all take a time-series approach to the examination of differential insider behavior — insider transactions

---

[7]It is recognized, however, that a plausible alternative explanation is that the passage of the 1984 act simply caused registered insiders to be more careful in hiding prosecutable actions.

volume is compared across regulatory eras. An alternative cross-sectional approach is to compare insider trading under two contemporaneous regulatory regimes. Masse, Hanrahan, and Kushner (1991) consider preannouncement takeover-related price runups for Canadian stocks that trade in different provinces. Since the penalties for insider trading vary widely across provinces in Canada, they posit that a finding of small (large) price runups in the strict (lax) province is consistent with the contention that insiders respond to increasing regulation. Their results are consistent with this hypothesis.

An Unresolved Question: The Importance of Outside-Insiders

The results cited in the previous section were obtained largely by examining the patterns of reported transactions of registered insiders prior over different time periods and around important firm events. In contrast to previous empirical research, the authors of these studies generally conclude that changes in the regulatory environment of the 1980s acted to deter registered insiders from taking advantage of their access to nonpublic information. However, the data indicate that both takeover premiums and the incidence of preannouncement runups in target firm share prices were as great (if not greater) at the end of the 1980s than they were at the beginning. If registered insiders were deterred by the increase in regulatory efforts, and if market anticipation does not provide a complete explanation of the runup phenomenon, then we must look for other factors to explain it. One possibility is that substantial preannouncement purchases may be attributable to the actions of those whose transactions do not appear in the Official Summary; i.e., those not employed by the firm. These outside-insiders include investment bankers, risk arbitragers, lawyers, accountants, financial printers and so forth — in short, anyone in possession of material nonpublic information of an impending takeover bid, other than the top-level executives of the firms involved.

A typical arrangement by which outside-insiders may profit from nonpublic information is provided in Keown, Pinkerton, Young, and Hansen, (1985).

> Antoniu [an employee in the M&A department of Morgan Stanley] would pass confidential information to Newman who subsequently would trade on the information and split the resultant profits with Antoniu. This scheme continued and

> expanded as Antoniu left Morgan Stanley in May of 1975 for a new position at Kuhn, Loeb, and Co. As Antoniu left Morgan Stanley, he enlisted the help of a remaining employee, E. Jacques Courtois, who thereafter passed inside information to Antoniu, who in turn relayed it to Newman to use in buying stock. The scheme expanded as Antoniu enlisted the help of two additional acquaintances to purchase stocks based upon Antoniu's inside information, and these accomplices in turn split their profits with Antoniu. To avoid arousing suspicion, the defendants established secret accounts with banks in Luxembourg, Switzerland, Bermuda, and the Bahamas. To further avoid detection, names were kept off all account statements; trades were made through multiple banks and brokers; payments to each other were made in cash, bearer bonds, treasury bills, or other nontraceable funds; personal meetings between the defendants were not allowed; and phone calls were disguised through the use of aliases.[8]

It is clear that, legal issues aside, the actions of outside-insiders might suggest an alternative explanation of price and volume runups contemporaneous with the observed reduction in trading by registered insiders.

Unfortunately, empirical evidence on the relative importance of transactions by outside-insiders is sparse. We return once again to the work of Meulbroek (1992). She employs as her sample a group of insider trading cases investigated by the Securities and Exchange Commission and points out the preponderance of outside-insiders among the defendants. She states that, over the time period covered by her study "few of the defendants in insider trading cases [were] corporate insiders required to report their transactions to the SEC. Only 24% of the defendants [were] employees (most of whom are not required to report their trades to the SEC) of the firms whose stock they trade" (footnote 11). Thus, while the empirical research to date has focused primarily on registered insiders, it is clear that insider trading has taken a new turn, and the accompanying research will require new techniques in the decades to come.

---

[8]Interestingly, the procedures described in this passage are not unlike those employed by Dennis Levine, and documented in Stewart's *Den of Thieves* (1992).

Summary of the Evidence and Directions for Future Research

If nothing else, examination of the steadily growing body of empirical literature on insider trading impresses upon one the important role information in the capital markets. It is clear that, at least until relatively recently, excess returns accrued to those with the most complete information sets. Implicit in this statement is the contention that, until recently, managerial motivations were discernible (ex post, if not ex ante) from their transactions in their own firms' shares.

If further advances are to be made, however, scholars must find ways to come to grips with some of the problems inherent in the extant research. First, the majority of the empirical research to date has employed the record of insiders' transactions as supplied by them to the regulatory authorities. While this approach may have been appropriate in a time when the likelihood of prosecution was minimal, the advent of increasingly severe penalties calls into question the accuracy of this database for many of the empirical questions to be considered. In the face of severe penalties rational insiders will either not trade or will attempt to disguise their actions.[9]

Along these lines, the use of alternative financial instruments (e.g., junk bonds) and strategies to profit from nonpublic information undoubtedly deserves greater attention. Cleeton and Reeder (1987) describe several combinations of stocks and options one might use to earn abnormal returns while minimizing the likelihood of prosecution. There is almost no empirical evidence on the extent to which individuals have used alternative securities to profit from nonpublic information and yet, few researchers (or regulators) would contend that insiders strictly limit their transactions to common stocks. Future research may require scholars to examine more closely transactions in other securities and other markets in order to gain a clearer picture of the changing nature and extent of insider trading.

Finally, the exploitation of nonpublic information by outside-insiders requires a great deal of research in order to identify a) the identities of these individuals, b) the nature of their transactions, and c) how

---

[9]For example, Cornell and Sirri (1992) note that several of the insiders involved in the Campbell Taggart case employed multiple brokers to hide their identities.

widespread outside-insider trading is. The latter point, of course, embodies significant (and complicated) legal, policy, and cost considerations. If the volume of aggregate insider trading has not been significantly reduced, just what has regulation accomplished? Cohen (1991) points out that the total cost of securities regulation approached $1 billion in 1991; as taxpayers and investors, we are obliged to ask whether we are getting our money's worth.

CHAPTER 6

PRICE AND VOLUME RUNUPS PRECEDING TENDER OFFER ANNOUNCEMENTS

In this chapter we present the results of an empirical investigation of transactions in the shares of tender offer targets in the period preceding public announcement of the offer. Tender offers provide an excellent event for the measurement of trading on nonpublic information because those in possession of such information can be fairly readily identified and because advance information virtually guarantees the possessor a substantial gain if it is utilized. Our results indicate that 1) abnormal returns and share volumes prior to tender offer announcements generally increased over the 1976—1990 period, while the regulatory environment became more restrictive; 2) preannouncement trading by registered insiders was not uncommon in the 1976—1984 period but declined significantly following the passage of the Insider Trading Sanctions Act of 1984 (ITSA); and 3) the imposition of increasingly stringent legal restrictions may have simply transferred insider trading activities from registered insiders, who are subject to disclosure requirements and fiduciary duties, to outside-insiders, who are relatively free from such scrutiny. Since insider trading by the latter group is notoriously difficult to monitor and even more difficult to prosecute in court, we conclude that existing anti-insider trading regulations are not effective in deterring insider trading in the aggregatee.[1]

This chapter extends the existing literature in several areas. First, insider trading around tender offers is examined from 1976 to 1990. The data from this period are especially rich due to the proliferation of takeover activities, which are associated both with the generation of nonpublic information and large security price changes. Furthermore, this period is unique because it is marked by the passage of increasingly comprehensive (and restrictive) legislation, a number of Supreme Court rulings dealing with insider trading-related issues, and increased

---

[1]This chapter is derived from empirical research performed by the authors over the 1988—1992 period.

enforcement activities by the SEC and the Department of Justice. As such, this chapter documents insider trading activities over five distinct regulatory eras characterized both by increasingly stringent penalties for those convicted of insider trading and by the increasing visibility of enforcement efforts.

The empirical results presented in this chapter suggest that increasing regulatory constraints have been reasonably effective in curbing preannouncement trading by registered insiders; we contend that the persistence of preannouncement price and volume runups is attributable to the action of outside-insiders.

Experimental Design

Until fairly recently, it has been assumed by many market professionals and academics professionals that trading on inside information is a fairly common (albeit illegal) activity undertaken by corporate officers and directors, despite the existence of regulations against it. Empirical tests of the early anti-insider trading laws using the data from 1950—1972 by Lorie and Niederhoffer (1968), Pratt and Devere (1970), Jaffe (1974a and 1974b), and Finnerty (1976a,b) focus on the trading of registered insiders and conclude that then-existing regulations were ineffective in deterring insider trading.

The recent wave of anti-insider trading laws started with the 1975 amendment to the Securities Exchange Act of 1934 that imposed both financial penalties of up to $10,000 and the possibility of imprisonment for up to five years for a person convicted of transacting in his/her corporation's stock on the basis of material, nonpublic information. This legislation signifies the first attempt by the regulatory authorities to deter insider trading by means of concrete civil and criminal penalties (although it should be noted that the act covers only inside-insiders). We have chosen this event as the starting date in our empirical examination.

In 1980 the United States Supreme Court ruled against the SEC in *Chiarella v. United States*,[2] which prompted the SEC to issue Rule 14e-3, which prohibits preannouncement trading by any person with access to material nonpublic information in the shares of firms involved in tender offers. This rule represents the beginning of the second

---

[2]Chiarella v. United States, 445 U.S. 222 (1980).

regulatory period in our study because it widens the scope of anti-insider trading regulations to include outside-insiders.

In August 1984 President Reagan signed the *Insider Trading Sanctions Act (ITSA)*,[3] which granted the SEC the authority to seek court orders for the disgorgement of profits amassed by inside traders, to bring civil suits against inside traders (independent of actions taken by the Department of Justice), and to impose fines of up to three times the profits obtained. The passage of this act signified the increasing zeal of the regulatory authorities in pursuing inside traders, and dramatically increased both the scope of the regulations and the penalties for those convicted of inside trading. As such, the enactment of this legislation constitutes the beginning of the third regulatory period in our empirical work.

The regulatory authorities started what is perhaps their most vigorous (and undoubtedly the most visible) campaign against insider trading with the arrest of investment banker Dennis Levine in May 1986. Levine's arrest was followed by the arrests of several others in various areas of the mergers and acquisitions business, along with the celebrated indictments of high officials at the investment banking house of Drexel Burnham Lambert, junk bond king Michael Milken, and several officials from the securities firm of Princeton-Newport, Inc., among others. We have chosen May of 1986 as the beginning of the fourth regulatory period because it has been contended that this wave of prosecutions sent a strong signal to market participants.

The enactment of the *Insider Trading and Securities Fraud Enforcement Act (ITSFEA)* in November 1988 marked the passage of the most restrictive anti-insider trading law to date. This act allows the government to pay informants a bounty of up to ten percent of the fine or the settlement to an informer; it increases the jail term to a maximum of ten years; imposes fines against investment firms that fail to supervise their staff and thereby prevent insider abuses; increases the maximum fines in criminal cases from \$500,000 to \$2.5 million; and allows investors who traded at the same time as the insiders to seek damages. Perhaps most importantly, this act requires that firms establish explicit anti-insider trading rules for their employees. The period from November 1988 to the end of 1990 constitutes the fifth and final regulatory era

[3]Public Law 98-376 (98th Congress).

investigated in the current chapter. The five regulatory periods are chronicled in table 1.

Hypotheses

The evolution of anti-insider trading laws and the increasing vigor of enforcement activities provide an opportunity to empirically examine the impact of these restrictions on trading by both inside-insiders and outside-insiders. The formal hypotheses to be tested are as follows:

Null Hypothesis:

> Anti-insider trading regulation has had no deterrent effect on insider trading.

Alternative Hypotheses:

1. Insider trading regulations have been effective in deterring insider trading by inside-insiders, and/or
2. Insider trading regulations have been effective in deterring insider trading by outside-insiders.

The Sample and the Data

The sample consists of 553 NYSE and AMEX firms that were the targets of tender offers between January 1, 1976, and December 31, 1990. Tender offers were chosen as the focal point of the investigation because they constitute a signaling device which effectively provides target shareholders a short-lived bounty (the tender premium) that disappears when the offer expires (Cohen 1990). As such, tender offer announcements are virtually always associated with substantial increases in target firm share prices upon the announcement of the offer, which makes trading prior to the event potentially profitable. As a result, the

Table 1
Major Events in the Recent History of Insider Trading Legislation and Prosecution

Regulatory Change	Effective Date	Descriptions
Amendment of the Securities Exchange Act (1934)	June 1975	Amended Section 32: Provides for fines up to $10,000 and imprisonment up to 5 years for those found to have traded on nonpublic information.
Amendment to the Securities Exchange Act of 1934	September 1980	Amended Section 14e: Prohibits trading based on nonpublic information about impending tender offers by anyone inside or outside of the firms involved.
Insider Trading Sanctions Act	August 1984	Amended Section 21: Imposes treble damages on any person trading on material nonpublic information; increased $10,000 fine imposed by 1975 Amendment to $100,000. Provides for civil suits by SEC.
Prosecution of Levine, et al.	May 1986	The arrest of Dennis Levine, which was followed by the arrests of many others involved in the mergers and acquisitions business signaled a dramatic increase in the vigor with which insider trading would be prosecuted.
Insider Trading and Securities Fraud Enforcement Act	November 1988	Imposes greater criminal penalties on inside traders, authorizes bounties for informants, provides for liability claims against inside traders by contemporaneous traders, and requires internal firm policies against insider trading.

tender offer is an event likely to be associated with insider trading. (The SEC's adoption of Rule 14e-3 suggests a regulatory view consistent with this contention.)

The sample was identified by examining every issue of the SEC *News Digest* published during the sample period and retrieving all firms listed as targets in 14D-1 (i.e., tender offer announcement) filings. From this initial sample, we then eliminated 1) firms not on the 1990 CRSP daily returns tape, 2) self-tenders, 3) subsequent bids in multiple-bid contests, and 4) firms that were mentioned in either *The Wall Street Journal* in a takeover-related context, or for which 13D filings were announced in *The Wall Street Journal* in the 60-day period preceding the tender offer announcement. The announcement date was defined as the earlier of the 14D-1 filing date or the announcement of the offer in *The Wall Street Journal*.

The Measurement of Abnormal Returns and Excess Volume

The first series of tests of insider trading activities involve the examination of abnormal or excess returns and excess share volume in the period preceding tender offer announcements over the five regulatory periods previously described. The existence of preannouncement runups in the prices and volumes of target firms' shares is assumed to be a necessary (but not a sufficient) condition for the existence of insider trading.

Large increases in stock prices are reflected in day-to-day returns in excess of what one would otherwise expect. For this study, we employ the market-adjusted returns approach as detailed by Brown and Warner (1985).[4] Daily excess returns are defined as returns greater or less than those on the market as a whole on a given day. Thus, for each target firm, daily stock returns and the daily returns on the CRSP equal-weighted market index were collected over a 151-day period

---

[4]Our use of the market-adjusted returns model is justified on the basis of Brown and Warner's (1985) simulation results suggesting that the residuals from various return-generating models are robust to model specification in the absence of mitigating circumstances (e.g., "event-date clustering"). None of the mitigating circumstances identified by Brown and Warner are present in our sample.

ending at the tender offer announcement date. The abnormal return for firm *j* on day *t*, AR(jt), is equal to

$$R(jt) - R(mt)$$

where R(jt) is the raw (i.e., observed) return for firm *j* on day *t* and R(mt) is the market return on the same day.[5] The portfolio excess return on day *t* is defined to be

$$AR(t) = \sum_{j=1}^{N(k)} AR(jt)/N(k)$$

where N(k) denotes the number of firms in the kth regulatory group (k = 1, . . . ,5). Under the null hypothesis of no abnormal stock price reaction, the daily test statistic, *t*, is equal to

$$AR(t)/S(AR(t))$$

where S(AR(t)) is the estimated standard deviation of the average daily abnormal returns over a 100-day estimation period ending 51 days prior to the event date. That is,

$$S(AR(t)) = [\sum_{t=-150}^{-51} (AR(t) - AAR(t))^2/99]$$

where AAR(t) is the mean daily abnormal return over the estimation period. Under the null hypothesis of no reaction, the test statistic is distributed as a Student *t*.

The analogous test statistic for intervals of greater than one day, t(CARt,τ), is equal to

---

[5]The return on stock *j* on day *t* is equal to [P(jt) + D(jt) - P(jt-1)]/P(jt-1), where P(jt) and P(jt-1) represent stock prices on days *t* and *t*-1, respectively, and D(jt) is the dividend paid on day t.

$$t_{(CAR,\tau)} = CAR(t,\tau)/((\sigma_{AR})(\tau - t + 1))$$

where t and τ represent the beginning and endpoints of the interval, and σ_{AR} is the abnormal return computed over the 100-day estimation period.[6]

If excess returns are attributable to information of an impending takeover bid, it is reasonable to believe that increasing preannouncement returns will be accompanied by increasing share volumes over the same period. Thus, daily share volume for each firm in the sample was collected from Standard and Poor's *Daily Stock Price Record* for the 100-day period preceding the announcement date.

Previous empirical work suggests that daily share volume (like daily returns) consists of components related both to overall market volume and to the firm. Thus, excess volume is defined as the residual volume remaining after that related to aggregate market movements has been accounted for. The basic volume variable employed for each firm is daily share volume as a proportion of outstanding shares. Following Morse (1981), Pincus (1983), and Richardson, et al. (1987), we constructed a standardized volume metric in the following manner.[7] Let

$$v(jt) = \frac{\text{Number of firm } j\text{'s shares traded on day } t}{\text{Number of shares outstanding for firm } j \text{ on day } t}$$

and

---

[6]Standard errors were calculated in the manner proposed by Leftwich (1981). Under the assumption of serial independence, the standard error of the N-day cumulative average residual is equal to the product of the standard deviation and the square root of N. The ratio of the cumulative average residual and the standard error provides a test statistic, which is distributed as a student t with N - 1 degrees of freedom.

[7]While our sample includes both NYSE and AMEX firms, the volume index includes only NYSE firms. This approach is consistent with the findings of Bamber (1986) who states "[m]y results suggest that Morse's (1981) concern about regressing non-NYSE firms' trading on a 'market' index including only NYSE firms may not be warranted, since I observed non-NYSE firms' trading to be more closely associated with NYSE firms' trading than with indexes based on either AMEX or OTC firms" (p. 41).

$$v(mt) = \frac{\text{Number of NYSE firms' shares traded on day } t}{\text{Number of shares outstanding for NYSE firms on day } t}$$

Excess volume is measured by the magnitude of the coefficient on a binary variable taking the value of 1/50 on each day of the event period (-50, -1), and zero otherwise, in the following OLS regression.[8]

$$v(jt) = a(j) + b(j)v(mt) + m(j)D(t) + e(jt) \qquad t=-100,-1$$

where

v(.t)	=	the percentage volume for firm *j* or the market on day *t*,
D(t)	=	a binary variable with a value of 1/50 for each of days -50 through -1, and zero otherwise,
a(j), b(j)	=	parameters identifying the intercept and sensitivity to market volume,
m(j)	=	the abnormal volume reaction during the event period, and
e(jt)	=	normally distributed error term.

The existence of abnormal volume will be reflected in statistically significant values of *m*.

We also examine intertemporal changes in total daily share volume as a proportion of outstanding shares. By computing both event and

---

[8]The use of a 50-day estimation period is somewhat arbitrary; however, the results of this work and others (e.g., Keown and Pinkerton (1981) and Pound and Zeckhauser (1990)) suggest that there is little evidence of pretakeover runups earlier than 50 days prior to the announcement of a takeover bid. Further, it should be noted that, to the extent that insiders do begin purchasing heavily in the estimation period, the resulting test statistics will be biased against the rejection of the null hypothesis.

estimation period values for this proportion for each target firm and netting the two, we obtained a measure of the change in preannouncement volume adjusted for firm-specific normal volume.

Measuring the Volume of Inside-Insider Trading

Next, we narrow our focus and examine the transactions of registered insiders in the sample firms. Registered insiders' transactions for the 100-day period immediately preceding the announcement were extracted from the Ownership Reporting System database compiled by the Securities and Exchange Commission and available through the National Archives. To qualify for inclusion in our sample, insider transactions must involve 1) direct ownership by the registered insider (that is, shares held by trusts or other indirect forms of ownership are excluded); 2) at least 100 shares; and, 3) open-market or private purchases or sales. (Shares acquired or disposed of via gifts or option or warrant exercise were excluded). Additionally, transactions must have been made by members of the board of directors, top-level executives, or large share holders.

As a gauge of the day-to-day transactions of inside-insiders, a daily index of the number of net purchase transactions was computed in the following manner. Let the number of net purchase transactions, NT(jt), of the shares of firm j on day t be defined as the number of (qualifying) purchase transactions less the number of (qualifying) sales transactions on that day. That is,

$$\mathrm{NT}(jt) = P(jt) - S(jt)$$

where P(jt) and S(jt) denote the number of purchase transactions and the number of sales transactions, respectively. Summing over all of the firms in the sample portfolio provides the total number of net purchase transactions on day t relative to the announcement date, which we denote NT(t). Summing the NT(t) values over t days provides a cumulative measure of all inside-insiders' transactions from the beginning of the event period to day *t*, which is denoted CNT(t).[9]

In the absence of preexisting trends in the data, randomization across firms and time periods would suggest that the expected values of both NT(t) and CNT(t) should be zero. Several researchers have found, however, that registered insiders are, on balance, net sellers. To account for the possibility that the data are skewed, we also computed a net cumulative insider trading metric, which is the difference between the value of CNT computed over the event period and the same statistic computed over the estimation period immediately preceding it. A positive value of this statistic suggests a preponderance of net purchases by registered insiders, adjusted for their normal pattern of transactions, while a negative value suggests the opposite. Both parametric and nonparametric comparisons of mean values are employed to determine whether 1) trading by registered insiders within regulatory groups is significantly different from the norm in the preannouncement period, and 2) the volume of inside-insider trading differs significantly across regulatory periods.

Empirical Results

Cumulative average abnormal returns (CARs) for the sample firms in each of the regulatory periods are reported in table 2.

The cumulative abnormal returns observed for the firms in our sample are striking due both to their magnitudes and to their patterns. By the announcement date, CARs exceeding 32 percent are observed for the subsample of firms in regulatory period V. Values of 27.55, 17.2, 19.25, and 29 percent are observed for the subsamples in periods I through IV, respectively.[10]

[9]The results of several recent empirical studies suggest the efficacy of similar statistics to measure insider trading volume. Notable among these are Penman (1982), Seyhun (1986), and King and O'Keefe (1986).

[10]With respect to the magnitudes of the announcement date CARs, our results are not dissimilar to those reported in several other studies, most notably Dodd and Ruback (1977) and Jensen and Ruback (1983).

Table 2
Preannouncement Cumulative Average Residuals for Tender Offer Targets During Selected Regulatory Periods

	Cumulative Average Portfolio Residuals				
Event Day	Period I: 1/76–8/80	Period II: 9/80–7/84	Period III: 8/84–4/86	Period IV: 5/86–11/88	Period V: 12/88–12/90
−50	0.0019	0.0013	0.0017	−0.0015	−0.0019
−40	0.0332	0.0070	0.0135	0.0190	0.0195
−30	0.0535	0.0239	0.0441	0.0239	0.0359
−29	0.0547	0.0260	0.0463	0.0210	0.0383
−28	0.0577	0.0327	0.0450	0.0250	0.0398
−27	0.0600	0.0335	0.0497	0.0243	0.0422
−26	0.0649	0.0316	0.0492	0.0257	0.0432
−25	0.0758	0.0290	0.0506	0.0282	0.0486
−24	0.0784	0.0289	0.0523	0.0331	0.0505
−23	0.0808	0.0298	0.0495	0.0357	0.0590
−22	0.0846	0.0323	0.0539	0.0381	0.0569
−21	0.0903	0.0332	0.0530	0.0426	0.0584
−20	0.0992	0.0368	0.0556	0.0501	0.0592
−19	0.1034	0.0373	0.0579	0.0637	0.0611
−18	0.1066	0.0389	0.0631	0.0638	0.0632
−17	0.1120	0.0410	0.0654	0.0688	0.0694
−16	0.1203	0.0458	0.0681	0.0707	0.0613
−15	0.1269	0.0539	0.0701	0.0734	0.0731
−14	0.1326	0.0593	0.0718	0.0765	0.0779
−13	0.1363	0.0599	0.0754	0.0836	0.0786
−12	0.1415	0.0649	0.0819	0.0848	0.0750
−11	0.1476	0.0673	0.0895	0.0898	0.0876
−10	0.1518	0.0678	0.0942	0.0932	0.0875
−9	0.1572	0.0713	0.0951	0.0983	0.0918
−8	0.1618	0.0732	0.1023	0.1026	0.0983
−7	0.1671	0.0781	0.1073	0.1072	0.1063
−6	0.1747	0.0852	0.1137	0.1155	0.1046
−5	0.1820	0.0899	0.1178	0.1290	0.1179
−4	0.1913	0.0990	0.1263	0.1508	0.1214
−3	0.2040	0.1103	0.1391	0.1808	0.1662
−2	0.2202	0.1239	0.1486	0.2034	0.1951
−1	0.2318	0.1410	0.1600	0.2304	0.2084
0	0.2755	0.1720	0.1925	0.2896	0.3235

Even more important, it is apparent that the pattern of rising abnormal returns begins long before the announcement, and continues through it. By the day immediately preceding the announcement, the CARs range from 14.1 percent (regulatory period II) to 23.2 percent (regulatory period I). This pattern of rising preannouncement returns is precisely what one would expect if information on the impending takeover bid is being impounded in securities prices prior to its public dissemination.[11]

We next compare excess returns and excess trading volume across regulatory periods. Panel A of table 3 reports, for each regulatory period, CARs computed over four intervals: (-10, -1), (-5, -1), (-2, -1), and (0). Given the results above, it is perhaps not surprising that all of the CARs are statistically significant at the ten percent level or better. More interesting, however, is the pattern of abnormal returns that emerges from our comparisons. Without exception, the CARs in periods IV and V exceed those in periods I, II, and III. In other words, the magnitude of preannouncement price runups has increased, rather than decreased, despite the existence of broader and more severe anti-insider trading regulation.

Explicit comparisons of interperiod differences in cumulative abnormal returns are reported in panel B of table 3. Under the null hypothesis, we would expect to observe no significant differences in CARs across regulatory periods. Conversely, effective regulations against preannouncement trading would be expected to deter those considering it, which, in turn, would be reflected in successively declining preannouncement CARs across periods. The values in panel B, however, suggest that abnormal returns in later periods exceed those in earlier ones. Consider, for example, the values of CAR(-10, -1). The period V value exceeds the period I value by 3.65 percent; the period V value exceeds those for periods III and II by 5.02 and 4.71 percent respectively. (All values are statistically significant.) Similar results are found in the comparison of the values in period IV to those of earlier periods.

On the other hand, we find few significant differences in the interperiod comparisons between periods V and IV, III and II, and periods II and I. In other words, CARs in the aggregate appear to be similar in magnitude in periods IV and V and in periods I, II, and III.

[11]The reader is reminded that preannouncement insider trading is only one of a number of possible explanations for this occurrence. Alternative explanations will be considered later in the chapter.

Table 3
Mean Excess Returns to Target Shareholders in Different Regulatory Periods

A. Daily average and cumulative average excess returns for selected subperiods

	Period I 1/76–8/80	Period II 9/80–7/84	Period III: 8/84–4/86	Period IV: 5/86–11/88	Period V: 12/88–12/90
CAR^{a}_{10}	.0843[e]	.0737	.0706	.1405	.1208
CAR^{b}_{5}	.0571	.0558	.0463	.1149	.1038
CAR^{c}_{1}	.0278	.0307	.0209	.0496	.0423
$\overline{X}\ R^{d}_{0}$	.0437	.0310	.0325	.0592	.1151

[a]CAR_{10} = cumulative average excess return from day -10 through day -1
[b]CAR_5 = cumulative average excess return from day -5 through day -1
[c]CAR_1 = cumulative average excess return from day -2 through day -1
[d]XR_0 = daily average excess return on the filing date
[e]Unless otherwise noted, all values are significant at the 10 percent level or better.

B. Interperiod differences in daily average and cumulative average excess returns

	Period V-IV	Period V-III	Period V-II	Period V-I	Period IV-III	Period IV-II	Period IV-II	Period III-II	Period III-I	Period II-I
CAR^{a}_{10}	−.0197[e]	.0502	.0471	.0365	.0699	.0668	.0562	−.0031[e]	−.0137[e]	−.0106[e]
CAR^{b}_{5}	−.0111[e]	.0575	.0480	.0467	.0686	.0591	.0578	−.0095[e]	−.0108[e]	−.0013[e]
CAR^{c}_{1}	−.0073[e]	.0214	.0116[e]	.0145	.0287	.0189	.0218	−.0098	−.0069[e]	.0029[e]
$\overline{X}R^{d}_{0}$	.0559	.0826	.0841	.0714	.0267	.0282	.0155	.0015[e]	−.0112	−.0127

[a]CAR_{10} = cumulative average excess return from day −10 through day −1
[b]CAR_5 = cumulative average excess return from day −5 through day −1
[c]CAR_1 = cumulative average excess return from day −2 through day −1
[d]XR_0 = daily average excess return on the filing date
[e]Indicated values are **not** significant at the 10 percent level.

We interpret the observed patterns of preannouncement excess returns as follows. First, preannouncement abnormal returns are at least as large in periods of more stringent insider trading regulation than in periods of less. Second, it is apparent from the patterns of excess returns immediately preceding the announcement that the magnitudes of preannouncement runups are increasing, rather than decreasing, with the advent of more vigorous regulation. Finally, the comparison of the later regulatory periods with the former suggests that events which occurred during period III may cause it to represent a "breakpoint" during which the nature of preannouncement insider trading activity underwent a substantive change. This possibility will be investigated further in subsequent sections of the chapter.

As a first pass at evaluating the magnitude of the excess volume preceding the announcement in each regulatory period, we employ the market model volume regression described previously. As noted, abnormal volume is reflected in the magnitudes of the regression coefficients on the dummy variable. The results of our examination of pre-announcement volume are reported in tables 4 and 5.

As shown in table 4, the average event period coefficients are positive and statistically significant in every regulatory period. That is, excess preannouncement volume in the target firms' shares persists across regulatory periods despite the passage of increasingly severe legislation and increasingly active enforcement by the regulatory authorities. The largest volume coefficients, .751 ($t = 5.43$) and 1.103 ($t = 3.06$) are found in the regulatory periods I and IV, respectively. The results indicate that, after adjusting for changes in total market volume, excess target firm volume was large and statistically significant in the 50-day period preceding the announcement in every regulatory period, consistent with the patterns of observed excess returns. Additionally, although excess volume fell off slightly in period V, the existence of large excess volume coefficients in both the first and fourth regulatory periods imply that total preannouncement target share volume was not generally reduced by increasing regulation.

The latter result is reinforced by the results of interperiod volume comparisons, as reported in table 5. Net daily share volume generally rises from regulatory period I through period IV, then drops slightly in period V. (The reader is reminded that net volume is daily event period volume net of estimation period volume.) T-statistics indicate that all of the volume values are significantly different from zero. To mitigate the

Table 4. Abnormal Volume Coefficient Estimates for Sample Firms in Each Regulatory Period[a]

Cell Number	Regulatory Period I			f^b	Regulatory Period II			f^b	Regulatory Period III			f^b	Regulatory Period IV			f^b	Regulatory Period V			f^b
1		<	−2.10	1		<	−2.10	1		<	−4.00	1		<	−3.15	1		<	−4.00	2
2	−2.10	–	−1.06	7	−2.10	–	−1.41	3	−4.00	–	−3.01	1	−3.15	–	−2.11	2	−4.00	–	−3.01	1
3	−1.05	–	− .01	39	−1.40	–	− .71	10	−3.00	–	−2.01	4	−2.10	–	−1.06	5	−3.00	–	−2.01	0
4	0	–	1.04	74	- .70	–	− .01	34	−2.00	–	−1.01	4	−1.05	–	− .01	36	−2.00	–	−1.01	3
5	1.05	–	2.09	23	0	–	.69	40	−1.00	–	− .01	15	0	–	1.04	40	−1.00	–	− .01	5
6	2.10	–	3.14	16	.70	–	1.39	22	0	–	.99	33	1.05	–	2.09	25	0	–	.99	18
7	3.15	–	4.19	7	1.40	–	2.09	5	1.00	–	1.99	11	2.10	–	3.14	7	1.00	–	1.99	10
8	4.20	–	5.24	2	2.10	–	2.79	3	2.00	–	2.99	4	3.15	–	4.19	6	2.00	–	2.99	5
9	5.25	–	6.49	1	2.80	–	3.49	3	3.00	–	3.99	3	4.20	–	5.24	4	3.00	–	3.99	3
10		>	6.49	3		>	3.49	3		>	2.99	4		>	5.25	9	4.00	>	4.00	2
Total				173				124				80				44				44
Mean Coefficient				.75				.29				.52				1.103				.403
T-Statistics				5.4				2.0				2.1				3.06				1.96

[a] Coefficients are estimated from the regression below:

v(jt) = a(j) + b(j)v(mt) + m.(j)D.(t) + e(jt)   t = −100, −1

v(.t) = the normalized volume for firm j or the market on day t,

D.(t) = a binary variable with a value of 1/T during the T-day event period and zero on every other day,

a(j),b(j) = parameters identifying the intercept and sensitivity to market volume,

m.(j) = the abnormal volume reaction during the first even subperiod,

e(jt) = normally distributed error term.

[b] f represents the frequency of the estimated coefficients in a specified range.

Table 5
Total Daily Share Volume as a Proportion of Shares Outstanding: By Regulatory Period

A. Net Daily Event Period Volume

	Period I	Period II	Period III	Period IV	Period V
Net event period share volume as a proportion of outstanding shares[a] (percent)	.824	.562	1.09	1.34	1.27
T- Statistic	7.31	4.42	5.80	3.81	3.17

B. Interperiod Comparison of Means

		Difference
Period V–Period IV	=	−.070
Period V–Period III	=	.180
Period V–Period II	=	.708[b]
Period V–Period I	=	.446[b]
Period IV–Period III	=	.250
Period IV–Period II	=	.778[b]
Period IV–Period I	=	.516[b]
Period III–Period II	=	.528[b]
Period III–Period II	=	.266[b]
Period II–Period I	=	.262

[a] These event period (−50, −1) values are net of estimation period (−100, −51) values.
[b] Significantly different from zero at the .05 level using Fisher's Least Significant Difference (LSD) test.

effects of possible skewness in the data (for reasons described earlier), in Wilcoxon Rank-Sum tests were also performed. The results further confirm the existence of significant volume increases from the estimation to the event periods in every regulatory period.

Panel B of table 5 reports the interperiod differences in the mean values reported above. An examination of all possible differences in means suggests that total daily share volume as a proportion of shares outstanding generally exhibits a pattern similar to that observed in the comparisons of abnormal returns. That is, after standardizing by dividing by outstanding shares, the average daily trading volume of target firms the later periods is significantly larger than that of target firms in the earlier periods, with a demarcation point in period III.

In sum, the evidence suggests that preannouncement runups in target firm share prices are associated with runups in the total volume of shares traded. Unfortunately, the results so far are aggregated in the sense that they deal with *total* returns and transactions volume. As such, they say little about who is (or is not) engaging in preannouncement trading. In the next section we seek to determine the source of this increase in volume by examining the transactions of registered insiders during the preannouncement period.

The Transactions of Registered Inside-Insiders

Prior research suggests that the number and size of transactions made by registered insiders are an efficacious measures of insider trading.[12] In table 6, we report the values of two such measures for each regulatory period. Panel A shows the average daily number of purchase transactions by inside-insiders in the 50-day event period ending one day prior to the announcement date net of those in the estimation period (day -100 through day -51). Panel B, on the other hand, reports the daily average volume of shares purchased by inside-insiders as a proportion of outstanding shares over the same period.

As shown in panel A, the daily average number of net purchases is positive and statistically significant in periods I and II: registered insiders were, on average, net purchasers in these periods. Beginning in period III, however, the net number of purchase values are all negative and not different from zero: the number of transactions of registered insiders in the period immediately preceding tender offer announcements indicates net selling, although the values are not significantly different from those in the normal (i.e., estimation) period.

---

[12]See, for example, Arshadi and Eyssell (1991).

Table 6

Inside-Insider Transactions Volume: By Regulatory Period

A. Number of Transactions	Period I	Period II	Period III	Period IV	Period V
Daily average number of net inside-insider purchases[a]	1.070	1.144	−.838	−1.203	−.611
T- Statistic	3.99	2.17	−1.13	−1.27	−.82
B. Volume of Shares					
Daily average number of (net) shares purchased by inside -insiders as a proportion of shares outstanding	.020	.003	−.0003	−.004	−.003
T-Statistic	2.27	2.17	−1.13	−.99	−1.01

[a] All inside-insider transactions measures are calculated for the event period (−50, −1) and are net of transactions in the estimation period (−100, −51).

Similar results are obtained when one considers net daily share volume of registered insiders as a proportion of the target firms' outstanding shares. Again we conclude that insiders were generally net purchasers prior to tender offer announcements which occurred in periods of relatively light regulation (periods I and II), but could not be definitively characterized as either net purchasers or sellers in periods of more stringent regulation and enforcement (periods III through V).

In sum, our results suggest the following. First, over the entire period studied, total target share volume prior to tender offer announcements displayed a marked tendency to rise, despite the passage of increasingly stringent regulations. Second, while this increase may be at least partially attributable to increased trading by registered insiders in the first two regulatory periods, measurement of inside-insider trading volume suggests that this was not the case in the latter periods. The volume results are consistent, therefore, with the patterns of excess returns observed. In the next section, we examine other explanations for the rising trend in total volume.

The Transactions of Outside-Insiders

The assessment of insider trading by outside-insiders poses a more difficult problem because of the inherent unobservability of the actions of the members of this group. As such, we utilize a series of tests which, taken together, facilitate inferences about the behavior of outside-insiders.

First, in each regulatory period we examine the preannouncement patterns of abnormal returns, and the volume of inside-insider transactions as a proportion of total share volume. Finding level or decreasing participation by inside-insiders across time periods (which would be reflected in flat or successively smaller proportions of total volume attributable to that of inside-insiders), would indicate that greater stringency of regulation has had a deterrent effect on the willingness or ability of inside-insiders to exploit their access to nonpublic information.

However, recent regulatory reforms have been aimed at insider trading generally, not just that attributable to inside-insiders. Thus, it is necessary to consider the possibility that total share volume is increasing while the portion attributable to inside-insiders is decreasing. We consider two potential causes for such a finding. First, as noted before, preannouncement price and volume increases may be the result of the workings of a perfectly legal market for information, as suggested by Jarrell and Poulsen (1987) and Jarrell, Brickley, and Netter (1988). Market anticipation is undoubtedly a factor in some cases; however, given our screening of the sample used in this research, we attribute a low likelihood to this explanation.

A second possible explanation for preannouncement price and volume increases is that market professionals (e.g., risk-arbitragers) have been able, acting on publicly available economic and financial information, to successfully predict that a given firm will become a takeover target. This view of risk-arbitragers as "superior security analysts" who are better able to weigh information than the rest of the market implicitly assumes that these individuals are in possession of a model that allows them to forecast accurately the probability that a given firm will become a takeover target. (In *Den of Thieves*, James Stewart indicates that this was the image Ivan Boesky strove to convey prior to his arrest. A reading of Boesky's book, *Merger Mania*, confirms this impression.)

Takeover prediction models received a good deal of attention in the empirical finance literature in the early 1970s due to their apparent ability to predict takeover targets using publicly available financial information.[13] Palepu (1986), however, notes that the existence of models that use published financial data to successfully pinpoint future takeover targets implies a paradox for those who believe in the informational efficiency of the financial markets.[14] He states that, earlier results notwithstanding, "the stock market does not seem to predict acquisition targets with a high degree of accuracy even three months prior to the announcement of takeover bids" (p. 3). His research indicates 1) the high predictive power displayed by the models developed in previous studies is largely the result of flawed sampling methodology, and 2) it is unlikely that one can consistently earn excess returns by predicting takeover targets using only publicly available information.

We test the robustness of the takeover prediction contention by replicating Palepu's study using a portion of our sample. Our test of its usefulness takes the form of a simple trading strategy. If the model is useful, we expect to observe for the portfolio of firms predicted by the model to become takeover targets a pattern of generally rising preannouncement excess returns. Conversely, those firms that the model fails to predict as targets should not display positive excess returns prior to the announcement. Although it is not possible to test every conceivable takeover prediction model, the inability of our model to generate excess returns will lead us to conclude that, as with UFOs, hauntings, and mind-readers, the burden of proof rests on those who contend that such things exist, rather than on those who are skeptical.[15]

---

[13]See, for example, Simkowitz and Monroe (1971) and Stevens (1973).

[14]According to modern financial theory, an informationally efficient market is one in which securities prices adjust rapidly to the arrival of new information. Langevoort (1992) provides an excellent discussion of the implications of, and recent developments affecting, the efficient markets hypothesis.

[15]Of course, the finding that any given model is not an accurate predictor does not preclude the possibility that there exists a better, albeit as-yet-undisclosed, model for the same purpose. Given that none has yet come

A related issue concerns the possibility that the costly acquisition of (legal) information regarding impending takeover bids may provide excess returns — in other words, the practice of classical risk-arbitrage. Larcker and Lys (1987) contrast risk-arbitrage and insider-trading below.

> Insiders obtain information as part of their managerial position (e.g., corporate earnings are known before they are released to the market). In contrast, Arbs obtain information by engaging in costly search activities (e.g., monitoring of organizations by hiring lawyers to provide expert opinions on antitrust issues). (p. 112, footnote 5)

Recent events suggest, however, that the ability to earn excess returns using only publicly available information may be more difficult than previously thought. The wave of insider-trading indictments of those involved in the mergers and acquisitions business generally, and risk-arbitrage specifically, along with the inability of researchers to find evidence of an effective takeover prediction model, suggests that many arbs in the period studied may have been more likely to fall into the category of outside-insiders than superior security analysts.

Ruling out the use of publicly available information leaves the exploitation of non-public information by inside-insiders, outside-insiders, or both as possible explanations for observed preannouncement price and volume runups. In the case of the former, we are able, as noted above, to track their transactions directly. Given persistent patterns of preannouncement abnormal returns and increasing share volume, and if we are able to rule out 1) increased trading by inside-insiders, 2) market anticipation, and 3) successful takeover prediction, we will conclude that the observed patterns are consistent with the existence of insider trading by those outside of the firm.

Methodology

To examine the contention that preannouncement price runups are attributable to market anticipation, we replicate Palepu's model using a

---

to light despite years of research, we are not uncomfortable with the conclusion that its existence is unlikely. Nonetheless, the reader is cautioned not to overinterpret the results of this test.

sample of 458 tender offer targets announced between 1976 and 1987. From this group, sufficient preannouncement financial data were available from the Compustat data base for 292 firms. Of these, 229 were the object of tender offers in the years 1975—1985; these firms were used in the estimation of the prediction model coefficients. The remainder (63 firms) were tender offer targets in 1986 and were used as a holdout sample; that is, for the assessment of the predictive power of the model.

The sample of nontarget firms whose data were used in the estimation process was randomly selected from the population of firms on the 1987 Compustat Annual Industrial tape. After screening for data availability, 293 firms remained. The number of nontargets used for the prediction stage was 1169. (Note: our sample sizes are roughly proportional to those of Palepu, who used samples of 163 and 256 targets and nontargets, respectively, for model estimation, and 30 and 1087 targets and nontargets for prediction.)

The following logistic regression model was estimated, using the 522 firms in the estimation sample:

$$IDT = b_0 + b_1AER + b_2GRDUM + b_3GROWTH + b_4LIQBAR + b_5INDDUM + b_6LEVBAR + b_7SIZE + b_8MTB + b_9P/E + b_{10}ROEBAR$$

where

IDT	=	1 if the sample firm was a tender offer target, 0 otherwise
AER	=	the average daily excess return on the firm's common stock for the three-year period preceding the announcement
GRDUM	=	binary variable designed to capture the existence of a resource mismatch likely to enhance the attractiveness of a potential target specifically; GRDUM = 1 if the sample firm has exhibited high growth, low liquidity and high leverage, or low growth, high liquidity, and high leverage, otherwise it is zero. ("High" and "low" values

refer to values greater or less than the population mean.)

GROWTH = the average annual rate of sales growth for the three-year period preceding the announcement

LIQBAR = the average value of the ratio of net liquid assets (cash + marketable securities less current liabilities) to total assets for the three years preceding the announcement

INDDUM = a dummy variable to capture the influence of "industry disturbances". Palepu notes the belief contends that takeover patterns exhibit an "industry effect"; thus the occurrence of a takeover in a given industry may increase the likelihood of future takeovers in the same industry. INDDUM is assigned a value of 1 if at least one firm with the same 4-digit SIC classification was acquired in the year preceding the observation year, and 0 otherwise.

LEVBAR = the average value of the ratio of long-term debt to book equity for the three years preceding the announcement

SIZE = the book value of total assets in the year preceding the event

MTB = the value of the ratio of the total market value of the firm's common equity to its book equity one year before the announcement

P/E = the value of the ratio of the market price of the firm's common stock to its earnings per share one year preceding the announcement

ROEBAR = the average value of the ratio of net income to total equity over the four year period preceding the announcement

(Note: all of the above ratios were calculated in the manner prescribed by Palepu (1986), Appendix A.)

Five versions of the logit model described above were estimated — a full model utilizing all of the variables, and four submodels using variable combinations identical to those employed by Palepu. The SAS procedure CATMOD was used to obtain maximum likelihood estimates of the parameters of each model.

Two of the resulting models have the highest (and virtually identical) likelihood ratios — model 2 (containing the AER, GRDUM, INDDUM, SIZE, MTB, and P/E) and model 3 (containing all variables but ROEBAR). Given the similarity in explanatory power, and given that model 3 is the same as that used by Palepu, we selected the latter for the purpose of estimating acquisition probabilities.

For each firm in the estimation sample, the acquisition probability, p^*, was calculated using the following formula.

$$p* = 1/(1 + .24e^{-Bx})$$

The constant preceding the exponential term reflects that proportion of the nontarget sample that was actually selected and used in parameter estimation. The term Bx represents a vector of coefficients and firm characteristics, as defined by the model. In our sample, the likelihood of selection for any given (nontarget) firm is .24.

Previous researchers typically used an arbitrary cutoff value (such as .50) to assign sample firms to the target or nontarget categories to assess the predictive power of the model. Palepu points out that this procedure makes the "results of prediction tests . . . difficult to interpret." Instead, the researcher must derive an optimal cutoff value "such that the marginal probability of observing [the acquisition probability] *p* if the firm is actually a target is greater than the corresponding marginal probability if the firm is a nontarget. The optimal cutoff probability is the value where the two conditional marginal densities are equal." (Palepu 1986, p. 14.)

The estimated acquisition probabilities for the firms in this study are reported in Table 7.

Table 7

Distribution of Estimated Acquisition Probabilities for Members of the Estimation Sample

Probability Estimate		Target Firms		Non-Target Firms	
Range	Mid-Range	Number	Percent	Number	Percent
0.000–.099	.05	15	6.6	110	37.5
.100–.199	.15	69	30.1	114	38.9
.200–.299	.25	131	57.2	51	17.4
.300–.399	.35	13	5.7	13	4.4
.400–.499	.45	0	0	2	.7
.500–.599	.55	1	.4	1	.4
.600–.699	.65	0	0	0	0
.700–.799	.75	0	0	0	0
.800–.899	.85	0	0	0	0
.900–.999	.95	0	0	2	.7
Total		229	100%	293	100%

Estimated acquisition probabilities range from zero to .99; however, as shown in table 7, only two exceed .60. Following Palepu, the range of estimated values is subdivided into ten segments and the midpoint of each segment is graphed against the frequency of occurrence to obtain an optimal cutoff value to separate predicted targets from firms not predicted to be targets by the model. For our sample, the cutoff value is .174.

Next we assigned the 1232 (1169+63) prediction year firms to predicted target and predicted nontarget groups on the basis of their estimated acquisition probabilities. As shown in table 8, the former group includes 398 firms, of which 27 were actually tender offer targets in

1986. The group of predicted nontargets includes 834 firms, 36 of which ultimately became targets. In other words, when only publicly available financial data were used to classify firms as tender offer targets, the model correctly identified only 42.9 percent (27/63) of the actual targets as such. Further, the model misclassified 31.7 percent (371/1169) of the nontarget firms as targets. In short, we find, as did Palepu, that the predictive ability of the model is small.

Empirical Results

The previous results notwithstanding, perhaps the acid test of any takeover prediction model is its ability to earn excess returns for its user. We next calculate the excess returns on the four portfolios described above: 1) all firms predicted as targets by the model, 2) actual target firms correctly identified by the model, 3) all firms not predicted as targets by the model, and 4) actual targets not predicted as such by the model. Cumulative portfolio residuals were calculated for each group for a 250-day period ending on the last day of the prediction year, December 31, 1986. The CARs for each portfolio are reported in table 8.

Both portfolios containing only the actual target firms display large positive excess returns of approximately similar magnitudes (38.75 percent and 40.84 percent for the targets classified correctly and those classified incorrectly, respectively). These are the returns one could have conceivably earned had one been in possession of an accurate takeover prediction model (or a crystal ball!). Lacking these, however, one would be unable to construct these portfolios *a priori*, given the current model's high rate of misclassification.

Instead, use of the model to classify firms would result in two portfolios: one group of predicted targets, which includes both actual targets and firms misidentified as such; and a group of predicted nontargets, which includes both actual nontargets and firms that actually became targets. For our sample, excess returns for the former portfolio are -4.44 percent; for the latter, -6.14 percent. Our results mirror those of Palepu: the model does not provide economically useful predictions. In the absence of evidence to the contrary, we conclude that, in efficient capital markets, the existence of such a prediction model is questionable, at best.

Table 8

Cumulative Average Portfolio Residuals for 250 Trading Days Ending 12/31/86 for Predicted Targets, Predicted Nontargets, and Actual Targets

	Predicted Targets		Predicted Nontargets	
Day	All Firms (n=398) CAR %	Actual Targets (n=27) CAR %	All Firms (n=834) CAR %	Actual Targets (n=36) CAR %
1	.14	−.11	.44	.11
10	1.13	3.97	1.19	5.96
20	−1.45	2.60	− .70	5.50
30	1.86	4.60	1.69	8.67
40	2.17	5.12	2.53	11.02
50	3.01	8.84	2.49	14.75
60	3.77	7.84	1.80	13.70
70	4.94	3.06	2.12	11.40
80	3.75	8.56	.97	16.38
90	4.12	8.83	− .24	16.34
100	4.06	7.25	− .99	13.81
110	2.06	8.99	−1.30	16.81
120	.81	8.33	−2.52	16.26
130	3.10	10.80	−2.14	19.45
140	4.94	15.92	−2.21	18.58
150	2.90	14.83	−2.99	20.75
160	−1.07	12.41	−4.34	20.96
170	2.44	16.05	−2.29	24.42
180	3.45	19.58	−1.97	29.02
190	1.29	22.20	−3.39	29.47
200	.60	25.10	− .08	29.16
210	−5.95	31.54	−8.26	31.81
220	−2.69	37.45	−6.17	40.21
230	−1.00	36.57	−4.63	39.33
240	−6.86	37.91	−8.59	39.83
250	−4.44	38.75	−6.14	40.84

Further Evidence

Given the persistence of preannouncement price and volume runups across time periods, a further implication of the outside-insider trading hypothesis is that, while registered insiders may have been deterred by the increasingly severe legal and financial penalties provided for under the new laws, outside-insiders (who, of course, are not required to report their transactions to SEC as registered insiders are) have not felt similarly constrained. A constant or a decreasing level of participation by inside-insiders across consecutive regulatory periods would be consistent with the suggestion that increasing share volume is attributable to trading by outside-insiders.

An empirical implication of the above is that the volume of trading by registered insiders, measured as proportion of total daily share volume, would display a secular decrease over the period studied. Panel A of table 9 reports inside-insider volume as a proportion of total daily share volume for each regulatory period.

Net inside-insider purchases as a proportion of total share volume fall from 1.54 percent in regulatory period I to -.412 percent in period V. (The reader is reminded that negative values reflect a preponderance of sales by registered insiders immediately preceding the announcement, net of normal transactions patterns.) The values of the test statistics indicate that, while the net purchases of registered insiders as a proportion of total daily volume are positive and statistically significant in the first two regulatory periods, this group became weak net sellers in the latter regulatory periods. Thus, the results are consistent with the hypothesis that the deterrent effects of increasing regulation resulted in lower participation by registered insiders.

Interperiod comparisons of the net purchase volume values (reported in panel B of the table) further bolster our contention that the trading pattern of registered insiders gradually reversed itself with the passage of time. The largest (and most statistically significant) differences in net purchase volumes are found in the comparisons of periods V and I, IV and I, III and I, and IV and II. Period III again appears to be a breakpoint between regulatory eras.

Summary and Conclusions

This chapter investigates insider trading activities prior to tender offers that were publicly announced over the 1976-1990 period. Our results suggest that preannouncement trading by registered insiders contributed to price and volume runups preceding tender offers in the

Table 9

Net Purchase Volume By Inside-Insiders as a Proportion of Total Share Volume: By Regulatory Period

A. Inside-Insider Volume

	Period I	Period II	Period III	Period IV	Period V
Net inside-insider purchases as a pro portion of total event-period share volume (percent)	1.540	1.323	−.347	−.611	−.412
T-Statistic	1.86	1.97	−1.46	−1.07	−1.11

B. Interperiod Comparison of Means

		Difference			Difference
Period II–Period I	=	−.217	Period V–Period IV	=	−1.023
Period III–Period I	=	−1.887[a]	Period V–Period III	=	−.065
Period IV–Period I	=	−2.097[a]	Period V–Period II	=	−1.735[a]
Period III–Period II	=	−1.670[a]	Period V–Period I	=	−1.952[a]
Period IV–Period II	=	−1.880[a]	Period IV–Period III	=	−.264
Period IV–Period III	=	−.021	Period IV–Period II	=	−1.934[a]
			Period IV–Period I	=	−2.151[a]
			Period III–Period II	=	−1.670[a]
			Period III–Period I	=	−1.887[a]
			Period II–Period I	=	−.217

[a] Significantly different from zero at the .10 level using Fisher's Least Significant Difference (LSD) test.

first two regulatory periods. In this sense, our findings are consistent with early studies of the phenomenon (e.g., Keown and Pinkerton 1981),with early studies of the phenomenon (e.g., Keown and Pinkerton

1981),as well as some of the most recent research in the field (see Meulbroek, 1992 and Cornell and Sirri, 1992).

The empirical evidence also strongly suggests that, in the face of increasingly stringent regulation and an increasingly vigorous regulatory stance by the SEC and Justice Department, preannouncement trading by registered insiders declined dramatically. However, insider trading *per se* did not disappear; rather, it appears to have simply shifted to outside-insiders, whose actions essentially replaced those of the registered insiders as contributors to preannouncement price and volume runups. An obvious explanation for this phenomenon lies with the disclosure requirements that are imposed upon registered insiders and which, of course, make it relatively simple for regulators to trace their actions. Transactions by outside-insiders, on the other hand, are more difficult to monitor and even more difficult to prosecute successfully in court. In this respect, our findings are generally similar and quite consistent with those of Seyhun (1992), who examines aggregate insider trading over a similar period and concludes that "[n]either the shareholders nor the statutes enacted during the 1980s seemed to provide additional effective constraints on insider trading." The problem seems to arise from the difficulty in containing the leakage of material information when profit opportunities are large, legal guidelines are vague, and the chance of (successful) prosecution is small. However, if the regulatory environment of the past 15 years is an indication, further regulation is unlikely to provide an effective remedy.

CHAPTER SEVEN

PUBLIC POLICY TOWARD INSIDER TRADING: A PROPOSAL FOR DECRIMINALIZATION

Publicly held corporations in the United States are subject to the most restrictive set of financial disclosure and insider trading rules in the world. In this chapter we provide an argument against prohibition of insider trading.

The most important aspect of corporate law involves regulation of securities transactions at federal and state levels. The accumulated rules and regulations could have presented the optimal volume of contracts if there were no transaction costs involving regulators' self-interests. Regulators, however, develop their own set of utilities that may be served via increases in regulation. For example, special interest groups actively lobby and receive a set of self-serving regulations in return for their financial and political support of the legislators. Regulatory agencies often act in concert with major private interest groups in promulgating and enforcing their rules (e.g., SEC and NYSE). This process of regulation and reregulation often results in significant accumulation of rules that may not be economically efficient for the regulated entities in general. Thus, corporate law that was originated as a means of lowering the transaction costs of producing explicit contracts may grow into a tangled, complex, repetitious and overly burdensome system of financial disclosure requirements and insider trading regulations. If so, a major overhaul in securities regulation is needed to bring the structure of corporate law in line with an economically defendable set of general provisions.

Besides the obvious incentive problems of the regulators in accumulating rules, there are other factors that necessitate reevaluation of the existing regulations. If positive transaction costs in market exchanges lead to the creation of modern corporations, drastic changes in technology and globalization of markets lead to reduced transaction costs that in return provide impetus to alteration of the regulatory structure.

The empirical evidence provided in the last chapter suggests the following observations with regards to the patterns of insider trading:

1. Despite six decades of anti-insider trading laws, transactions based on material nonpublic information have continued,
2. The profitability of insider trading has increased over time,
3. Registered insiders whose trading is required by law to be disclosed regularly to the SEC have abstained from illegal trading at least in their own names,
4. With the abstention of registered insider trading and exclusion of other legal forms of trading based on material nonpublic information, the evidence strongly supports the contention that insider trading has merely shifted from registered insiders to outside-insiders without a discernable decline in total volume.

The remainder of this chapter defines the identities of insiders, examines property rights in information, provides a critique of arguments against insider trading, and presents the rationale for decriminalization of insider trading.

The Identities of Insiders

Registered Insiders

Section 16 of the 1934 act attempts to discourage corporate insiders from using privileged information in their stock trading. Section 16a required officers, directors and every person who directly or indirectly owns ten percent of a class of equity securities registered under the act to file a report with the SEC at the time this status is acquired and at the end of every month in which ownership of such securities is altered due to purchase or sale.

The title *officer* refers to president, vice president, secretary, treasurer or financial officer, comptroller, or principal accounting officer, or any person who perform such functions. The term *director* refers to an individual who is a member of the board of directors that is established to meet the requirement of the state chartering agencies. The *beneficial owner* of ten percent is defined by the SEC as a person who holds securities in the name of his or her spouse and their minor children. Registered insiders become privy to material nonpublic information either through job-related information exposure or through their significant ownership position.

Temporary Insiders

This label applies to parties that are not directly employed by the firm but because of a temporary position that they hold may become privy to material nonpublic information. Such individuals include investment bankers, attorneys, and accountants who provide services to the firm and have access to inside information because of their positions. The definition for temporary insider was established in *Dirks v. SEC.*[1] Footnote 14 of the opinion stated that

> Under certain circumstances, such as where corporate information is revealed legitimately to an underwriter, accountant, lawyer, or consultant working for the corporation, these outsiders may become fiduciaries of the shareholders. The basis for recognizing this fiduciary duty is not simply that such persons acquired nonpublic information, but rather that they have entered into a special relationship in the conduct of the business of the enterprise and are given access to information solely for corporate purposes . . . For such a duty to be imposed, however, the corporation must expect the outsider to keep the disclosed information confidential, and the relationship at least must imply such a duty.

Tippees

A tippee is not an insider to the firm but receives material nonpublic information from either a registered or a temporary insider. While the liabilities of registered and temporary insiders arise from their fiduciary duties towards shareholders, tippee trading does not violate, at least directly, any fiduciary responsibilities. Tippees are not, after all, fiduciaries. In Cady, Roberts & Co.,[2] a director tipped the inside information to a broker who subsequently traded for his clients. The SEC described two key elements to identify the liability in the case: 1) the existence of a relationship affording access to inside information

---

[1]463 U.S. 646(1983).

[2]40 SEC 907 (1961).

intended only for corporate use and 2) the unfairness of allowing a corporate insider or its tippee to take advantage of the inside information before disclosing it.[3]

The question of tippee liability was further explored in two related cases. In the first case, Investors Management Co.,[4] the SEC brought administrative action against institutional investors who sold Douglas Aircraft Co. stock after being tipped on a downward revision of estimated earnings by Douglas. The tipper in this case was Merrill Lynch Pierce Fenner & Smith, which was the investment advisor for Douglas in a debenture issue. The SEC argued, as it had done in Cady Roberts, that tippee liability is appropriate whenever the tippee knows or has reason to know that the information being used in trading is nonpublic and has been distributed improperly and on a selective basis. The focus is again on the tippee being in a position of access to inside information. While concurring with the decision, Commissioner Richard Smith favored making the liability conditioned upon whether the tippee knew that the information received was in breach of a duty by a person having a special relationship to the issuer not to disclose the information.[5]

In the second tippee case, *Shapiro v. Merrill Lynch Pierce Fenner & Smith*,[6] a private class action suit was brought against Merrill Lynch for the sale of Douglas stock. The court ruled that Merrill Lynch and its tippees had the same liabilities as the insiders to the firm by virtue of the special access they had to inside information. Therefore, in tippee cases, access, rather than fiduciary duty was at issue.

Outside-Insiders: Risk Arbitragers

Arbitrage refers to simultaneous purchase and sale of assets in two different markets when there are temporary discrepancies in prices between markets. As the market for corporate control activities exploded

---

[3]Id. at 912.

[4]44 SEC 633 (1971)

[5]44 SEC at 649-650.

[6]495 F.2d 228 (2d Cir. 1974).

in the 1970s and 1980s, the magnitude of risk-arbitrage activities reached an all time high.

While risk-arbitrage is not limited to takeover cases, such transactions provide significant profit opportunities for risk arbitragers (arbs). The business of risk-arbitrage involves examining legal, financial and tax information on prospective targets to assess the likelihood of a successful takeover. If the likelihood is within an acceptable range, the arb takes a long position in the securities of the target firm and an offsetting short position in the shares of the bidding firm.

Brown and Raymond (1986) present a model to predict the probability of a successful takeover:

$X = (P_{mt} - P_f) / (P_{Tt} - P_f)$, where
X_t = takeover probability
P_{mt} = prevailing market price
P_f = price if tender offer fails
P_{Tt} = tender offer price

Suppose that the market price of the target share six weeks before the public announcement of tender offer was \$40 and the tender offer is for \$60. Further assume that upon the announcement of the tender offer the price of the share increases to \$55. The probability of success in takeover according to this model is (55 - 40) / (60 - 40) = 75%. On the other hand if the market price after the announcement moves only to \$45 then the probability of success is (45 - 40) / (60 - 40) = 25%. Brown and Raymond show that for completed takeover cases the probability never drops below 70%. The market price, therefore, significantly discriminates between eventual outcomes. The authors further demonstrate that while the probability of success in risk arbitrage is dependent upon unsystematic event risk rather than systematic market risk, market prices do provide the correct signal.

The probability of a successful takeover is increased when the investment banker leaks the news of the acquisition efforts to the arbs. The information leakage allows the arbs to acquire, on short notice, a significant quantity of the shares of the target firm. Consequently, the investment banker could round up a large number of shares needed for a successful takeover from a relatively small number of arbs who are interested in unloading their positions for a premium. The bidder is willing to pay substantial premiums over the prices that arbs have paid in order to take rapid control of the target before its managers could launch a vigorous antitakeover strategy. The information leak by the investment banker, and the effective stock parking by the arbs increases the probability of a successful takeover. If takeovers are socially useful activities then information leaks and stock parking are justifiable conduct.

But what sounds like an economically justifiable transaction often falls in the realm of insider trading. To make the issue more clear, let us examine the organizational structure of investment banking firms. Within any given investment banking firm there is the notion of a "Chinese wall" separating investment banking activities such as mergers and acquisitions from its in-house arbitrage activities. The Chinese wall rule is designed to prevent the leakage of information from the M&A group (whose responsibilities include advising their clientele (bidders and/or targets) on takeover-related matters) to the arbitrage group (whose main task is to purchase shares of the prospective targets). Despite the usual research efforts in risk arbitrage involving legal matters such as the antitrust issue or financial position of the target, the most valuable information for a profitable arbitrage is nothing other than a good tip on a forthcoming tender offer. So the arbs are looking for good tips that the M&A group is privy to. The Chinese wall may be effective on the surface because of the relative ease in getting caught by the SEC if M&A group openly exchanges information with the arbs in the same firm. But the M&A and arb groups could easily barter information with similar departments in other investment banking firms.

One such example could demonstrate the situation. In 1984—1985 Martin Siegel was the head of M&A department at Kidder, Peabody & Co. while Robert Freeman was the head of the arbitrage group at Goldman Sachs. Despite the existence of a Chinese wall, Siegel was instrumental in establishing the newly initiated arbitrage department in Kidder, Peabody & Co. Siegel repeatedly exchanged material nonpublic information on mergers and acquisitions activities of his clients with Freeman who used the information for arbitrage trading in Goldman Sachs. In return, inside information that Freeman was receiving from Goldman Sachs's M&A department was routinely passed to Siegel and subsequently to the arbitrage group in Kidder, Peabody, & Co. To avoid drawing any attention to their activities, the arbs at Kidder, Peabody, & Co. traded through third party brokers, such as Boyd Jefferies, whose specialty was trading on third market or off market. While subsequent indictments of both Siegel and Freeman on insider trading charges made these activities public, it is reasonable to assume that such information swapping is prevalent on Wall Street.

In sum, the business of risk-arbitrage depends upon collecting material nonpublic information. Because of the large magnitude of event-related unique risk in arbitrage transactions, the most reliable, and hence most profitable transactions are those conducted based on tips of inside information. An effective anti-insider trading campaign would likely involve closing down the business of risk-arbitrage.

Investment Bankers and Attorneys Who Are Not Temporary Insiders: Institutional Investors

As is the case with Wall Street, financial activities are generally concentrated in condensed geographic areas. Furthermore, improvements in the quality and costs of telecommunications technology link various markets together through electronic mail and other devices. This creates an environment characterized by formal and informal informational links and exchanges. The flow of information among market participants such as investment bankers, attorneys and the management of institutional investment firms is a well known fact. Such information bartering has been part of the business of securities transactions for a long time. The whole notion of rumors on the street and their effectiveness in moving stock prices significantly attests to the fact that material, nonpublic information is difficult to contain.

With information asymmetry ever present, firms often have incentives to disclose material nonpublic information, albeit confidentially, to financial intermediaries including commercial banks, insurance companies, and mutual and pension funds. There are many cases in which such assumably confidential disclosure is not kept as such, leading to widespread rumors and speculations (e.g., the case of Bank of Boston).

Property Rights in Information

The notion of property rights refers to the range of privileges that asset holders are entitled to including the rights to possess, use, manage, receive income, exclude nonowners from access, transfer the use of the asset, waive, abandon or sell the asset.[7] Property rights are defined through informal arrangements based on customs, or on formal arrangements specified in constitutional provisions, statutes, and court rulings.

In the absence of a specific property rights assignment, the asset belongs to a common pool of users. While the assignment of property rights generally leads to a more efficient use of the asset and hence to its value maximization, common pool access is potentially wasteful (e.g., Gordon 1954). Under this argument, the private cost of using the asset is less than its social cost, and there will be overusage of the asset. The reason for the overusage is because the user decides on the total quantity by equating only part of the marginal cost (the private marginal cost) to the marginal return. Since social marginal cost is greater, the overproduction is inevitable.

Common pool access also increases the cost of allocation of the asset to the higher-value user and hence reduces the value of the asset. Demsetz (1967) contends that the assignment of property rights is a prerequisite for market pricing of the assets based on supply and demand conditions among economic agents. Such a pattern is currently observed in the transition of eastern European countries from centralized economies to decentralized price-making markets.

Assignment of property rights leads to an efficient system of exchanges among economic agents (Alchian and Demsetz 1973). In "the problem of social cost" Coase (1960) shows that if transaction costs of property rights acquisitions, subdivisions, and combinations were zero, there would have been no need for law because individual economic agents could have negotiated their property rights without any disputes. In such an environment there is no need for economic institutions. The law, however, exists because transaction costs in allocation and reallocation of property rights is positive. The provisions stated in the law, in lieu of private contracts, include general standards that contracting parties oblige themselves to follow. As we argued earlier, the law provides a cost-efficient alternative to explicit contracting of general provisions that are applicable for all parties. Those who legislate the laws (politicians), and those who supervise their applications (the courts) face special interest groups whose interests are affected by

---

[7]A. M. Honore, "Ownership," in A. G. Guest, ed., *Oxford Essays in Jurisprudence (First Series)* (Oxford: Clarendon Press, 1961), pp. 107—147.

provisions of the law. The self-interest of the legislators and judges enters into the realm of property rights institutions along with various property rights holders.

Historically, it has been shown that when special interest groups are in a position to successfully affect the decisions of the legislators and judges for their own benefit, economic development and efficiency are undermined. Friedman (1985) described the early nineteenth-century American legal environment as one with a clear objective of promoting economic development and expanded markets. By the late nineteenth century, however, the law became more concerned with special interest groups who lobbied for position and power in society. This leads to smaller economic expansion and lower efficiency.

When the existing property rights arrangements become incompatible with new developments in the economy due to changes in relative prices, technology and regrouping of special interest groups, there will be incentives for change. This will manifest itself in the form of economic agents adopting new property rights arrangements and the mutation of the old system for the purpose of seeking new profit opportunities.

The property rights assignments in information follow a similar pattern. In recent years there have been significant changes in the following factors that necessitate a reexamination of existing rules:

1. The relative prices of the information produced
2. The state of information production and dissemination technology
3. The demand for regulatory changes in dissemination of information.

The first two factors are market forces that would increase the returns to new parties if property rights are reassigned. With the proliferation of takeover activities and the resulting surge in new ventures such as risk arbitrage, the demand for information has increased significantly. The value of information has also increased drastically reflecting substantial premiums that can be earned if the crucial information is attained. The insider trading profits of the 1980s were the largest in the history of such transactions. The increase in anti-insider trading laws, vigorous enforcement activities, and the evolution of case law have created an environment of uncertainty as to consequences of inside information production and subsequent trading. The property rights assignment of information is vague at best, requiring new analysis. The notion of market efficiency that is critically dependent upon the production and dissemination of information is greatly undermined due to legal ramifications of inside information production and its use in trading. Reassignment of property rights in information has the potential for the allocation of the information to its highest value user.

Technological advancements in information production and dissemination also affect the property rights institutions. With substantial improvements in information technology, the transaction costs of information production are reduced significantly. Telecommunication advancements have significantly reduced the cost of telephone communications, fax links, and electronic mail systems. Small and powerful computers provide ready access to price data in various global stock exchanges instantaneously. The multiple listing of stocks in international exchanges allows for 24-hour-per-day trading on a large number of stocks. Therefore, the price information in one market is disseminated to other markets with awesome speed. Technological advancements along with intensification of competition in the telecommunications and computer industries lead to an environment in which information is produced faster and cheaper than ever, making its containment very difficult. Furthermore, the globalization of the economy and relative uniformity in the prices of the same securities in various markets limit the impact of country-specific regulatory restrictions on information dissemination.

The role of regulatory agencies is the third important factor to examine. The regulatory system is supposed to promote economic development and efficiency. But special interest groups lobby legislators and politicians to pass provisions that serve special interests while harming others. Peltzman (1976) contends that politicians respond to the demands of special interest groups in an effort to get votes and other forms of political support. This in turn affects the outcome of the property rights institutions and the distribution of wealth. New reallocations may take place based on the significance of the political support the new special interest groups provide. Currently the U.S. provisions of property rights distribution are stated in the Constitution, common law, legislative and judicial law. Politicians respond to the demand for statutory adjustments that address the prevailing expectations and resist those that involve the violation of the established precedents.

In the case of information production and dissemination, legislators, courts, and the SEC are important players. As one of the important special interest groups the New York Stock Exchange actively lobbies

Congress for desirable legislation and the SEC for its enforcement purposes. The SEC and NYSE have served their mutual interests by working together on a variety of regulatory and enforcement activities.

Arguments Against Insider Trading: A Critique

The Property Rights Argument

A recurring theme to insider trading is the argument that such trading is based on the misappropriation of valuable property (information) from its owners (e.g., the firm) by the insider (e.g., Easterbrook 1981, and Scott 1980). Following the contracting literature we define the firm as a nexus of contracts among stockholders, bondholders, and managers. Since no one has suggested that bondholders should be assigned the property rights, the main debate is whether the property rights should be assigned to the shareholders or the managers. Easterbrook suggests that managers should not be assigned the property rights to information because that will make "proper" trading inseparable from "improper trading." Proper trading is argued to include purchase of securities by the managers in the process of their employments in the firm in order to align their self-interest with that of the shareholders. The argument is drawn from the literature on managerial compensation that suggests that share ownership by managers contributes to the mitigation of stockholder-manager conflict (e.g., Diamond and Verrecchia 1982).

According to Coase (1960), the property rights to information should be assigned to the highest-value user. Managers and shareholders negotiate to determine if the property rights to information are more valuable for managers or for shareholders. If the highest-value user is the shareholder group, it would be expected that the negotiation between two parties would lead to the assignment of the property rights to shareholders. This would create voluntary rules banning insider trading by managers. One might logically ask, then, why stockholders have not pressed for such a ban if they are truly fearful of management actions.

The question also arises as to why is it necessary to deter insider trading through legal statutes as opposed to individual contracting within the firm. No one has suggested regulation of the way compensation packages are designed between managers and the firm. If such elements can be individually contracted why should the assignment of property rights be any different?

It may be argued that Coase's allocation of property rights assumed no transaction costs. If there are significant transaction costs associated with writing explicit contracts banning insider trading and their enforcement at the firm level, there may be justification for a legal ban on such trading. Easterbrook argues that contracting through the law is more efficient in both its contracting cost and its enforcement efficacy. This argument presumes that shareholders would have demanded anti-insider trading measures at the firm level if there were no legal provisions prohibiting it. A legal ban, the argument follows, is less expensive, and therefore more efficient. There is, however, no evidence to prove this. Prior to the passage of *The Insider Trading and Securities Fraud Enforcement Act of 1988,* there were no widespread voluntary adoptions of provisions banning managers from insider trading in the corporate charter or managerial employee contracts. The 1988 act required public corporations to adopt explicit policies to police employee insider trading. This seems to be in contradiction with Easterbrook's argument that the demand of corporations for a cost-efficient form of contracting brings about inclusion of such provisions into the law.

Furthermore, it is unlikely that firm-specific contracts are costly or difficult to enforce. If sensitive material nonpublic information is available only to a few top executives, the employee contracts of such executives could include provisions banning them from using such information for personal trading if shareholders so desire. Those who violate the rule would face various penalties including termination of employment and forfeiture of the profits. Since no such evidence exists to justify promulgation of the 1988 act, it is safe to assume that the rule is inefficient. Legal rules requiring corporations to have anti-insider trading provisions in the corporate charter prevent the firms from making a choice in property rights assignments.

The Issue of Fairness

This argument contends that information used in trading is unfairly stolen from others (e.g., shareholders) who have invested in the production of information. Furthermore, the argument goes, insider traders are at a competitive advantage in trading because of their superior information.

The fairness argument relies on the belief that those trading in the market should have equal access to information. An extreme example of this argument is presented by Stanley Sporkin, the one-time chief of the SEC's enforcement division (Herzel and Katz 1987). He provided a hypothetical scenario in which an investor sees from the window of a landing airplane that the main plant of a company is on fire and immediately calls his broker to sell the shares of that company. According to Sporkin this should be illegal since the trader has more information about that company than almost every other shareholder. While this extreme opinion is not shared by all of those who object to insider trading, it shows the extent to which this line of argument may be taken if we demand equality of information for shareholders.

The amount of information various shareholders hold regarding a given company is never equal. For example, security analysts have far greater amounts of public and private information about a given company. They accumulate significant amounts of publicly available information by studying the trends in the economy, the industry, and the firm. They further discuss issues of importance with the top level executives of the companies who often quite willingly provide important sensitive information to the analysts. The executives do not disclose the information for their own personal benefits but for the benefit of bringing the share prices to their true value and to resolve the information asymmetry problem. This has been a common practice. Now what will the analyst do with this kind of information that has been acquired by spending significant amounts of time and resources? The analyst will use the information for trading shares for its clients. The clients pay commissions for the analyst for exactly that reason: they have collected important and material information. Is not this kind of trading a form of insider trading under the fairness argument? Yet, this practice seems to have been tolerated by the SEC, for the most part.

Another scenario may also be instructive. Suppose that an acquisition group has been studying the prospect of acquiring a firm. The primary search for value in acquisition "is not a matter of private information but to a great extent private interpretation of public information on the target juxtaposed with private information about the acquisition group, its special needs, goals and ability to control timing" (Shubik, 1985, pp. 37—38). The information that the bidding group has is obviously very unique and is not expected to be at the same level as another shareholder of the target company. To successfully acquire the firm the acquisition group and its investment banker decide to share their intentions with other investors (e.g., risk arbitrager) who in turn purchase a large number of shares in the target firm. The success of the takeover plan is critically dependent upon speedy acquisition of a controlling share. The arbitragers play an important role by selling their shares to the bidder for a premium. If takeovers are socially desirable transactions that improve efficiency,[8] then the process of a successful acquisition should be treated the same way. The bidder and its investment banking advisors have voluntarily disclosed their intentions to risk arbitragers because it is in their best interests. Why should bidding agents share their private interpretation of the target value and their intentions in acquiring the target with other shareholders as the notion of equality in information and fairness suggests?

In sum the unfairness argument does not hold when considering open market transactions. A person who has received inside information may decide to take one of the following three actions: 1) to release the information then trade; 2) to trade first and then release the information; or 3) to do nothing. Suppose a shareholder has filed a sell order with his/her broker on that share. Regardless of the insider's choice of action, the sell order will be executed. If the insider chooses the first alternative the price will move up (assuming that information is positive) and the seller may receive a premium depending on how fast the information is reflected on the price. The insider, however, does not receive any benefits from this strategy. Option two, however, provides profits for the insider while increasing the share price. Again the seller is going to benefit, to some degree, because the trading by the insider may itself provide the right signal to the market about the news. If the insider is effectively prohibited from trading before the release of the material information, there is no guarantee that the information will be released at all because he/she may choose to do nothing. To the extent that information release is critical to market efficiency, this outcome is not desirable. Now if information is not released, the seller will receive a price potentially less than the price paid if the insider was following option two, trading before the disclosure of the information. In this scenario, the fairness argument fails to provide an economically justifiable reason to prohibit insider trading.

The legal perspective on the notion of insider trading being unfair is that it is unjust. Nozick (1974) presents a popular theory of justice as the absence of coercion. Accordingly, "acts between consenting adults are just. Individuals or governments who prevent such acts are acting unjustly, and individuals who commit acts that aggress against others,

---

[8]Literally hundreds of empirical studies in finance bear out this contention.

except in self defense, are acting unjustly" (McGee, 1988, p. 36). If an individual takes the property of another without that person's consent (e.g., misappropriation of information) a governmental agency (e.g, the SEC) may step in to prevent the coercive takings. As suggested by a former SEC Commissioner (Karmel) such power in the hands of an agency such as the SEC may become abusive. An alternative to SEC interference is the protection provided to the property owners in common law and tort law.

While the fairness argument is one of the most frequently cited factors against insider trading, it fails to provide a convincing economic analysis.

Effects On Bid-Ask Spreads and Liquidity

The theoretical literature against insider trading also includes arguments that informed trading results in wider bid-ask spreads (e.g., Bagehot 1971, Copeland and Galai 1983, Glosten and Milgrom 1985, Kyle 1985) and reduced liquidity (e.g., Glosten 1989, and Leland 1992). In this literature the market is assumed to contain three categories of traders: liquidity traders, informed traders, and market makers. Liquidity traders' transactions stem from their need to purchase goods and services in the market. The transactions of this group do not have a particular strategic pattern related to the capital market other than their needs for liquidity. Informed traders are those who are in possession of material nonpublic information (i.e., inside traders) whose trading causes significant price changes. The market makers set the prices in each period and take positions as necessary to meet the supply and demand requirements.

This literature argues that when an order to buy or to sell a block of securities is submitted, the market maker can determine whether or not the order is from an informed insider by either the size of the order (Easley and O'Hara 1987, Hasbrouck 1988) or time of day (Harris 1986, Admati and Pfleiderer 1988). The choice of trade size and time of day is motivated by the informed trader's intention to keep material nonpublic information from the public to guarantee insider profit.

The theoretical conjecture is that when the market maker identifies the source of the order as an informed trader, the increase in price due to the buy order will be greater than when the order is from noninformed traders. Conversely, when the order to sell is deemed to be from an informed trader, the market maker cuts the price deeper than usual with the expectation that the insider trade is based on material nonpublic information. The affect on liquidity is reasoned similarly.

Liquidity is defined as the number of shares traded for a given adjustment in price. When the buy order is perceived to be from an informed trader, the increase in price is greater than normal for the quantity that is ordered. This steeper than usual increase in price reduces the demand for further purchases, therefore, reducing liquidity. If the order is to sell, the reduction in price is greater than usual reducing the number of shares ordered to be sold. Again this leads to reduced liquidity. Sirri (1991) and Gammill, Sirri, and Fleming (1992) find empirical support for the prediction that market makers increase their sensitivity to the order flow as the likelihood of informed trading increases, and for the effects of trade size on bid-ask spreads.

Cornell and Sirri (1992) examine insider trading surrounding acquisition of Campbell Taggart by Anheuser-Busch in 1982. News of the impending takeover was leaked by one of Anheuser-Busch's directors to a group of individuals who proceeded to purchase the shares of Campbell Taggart. The identities of inside traders were subsequently identified in the criminal and civil litigation that followed the event. The authors used the court records to isolate individual insider transactions from other trading in market. This allows for the analysis of individual insider transactions within the trading day in contrast to most other insider trading research that rely on daily transactions. The authors report the following results: 1) insider transactions bid up the price of Campbell Taggart share significantly; 2) insider trading did not result in widening of bid-ask spreads and; 3) market liquidity actually *increased* while insiders were trading. The increase in share price due to insider trading is consistent with more recent empirical literature (e.g., Meulbroek 1992). However, the results on bid-ask spreads and liquidity dispute the arguments presented in the theoretical literature reviewed earlier.

The results also dispute the notion that the market contains only three parties (liquidity traders, informed traders, and market makers). The authors present noise traders as active participants in trading (see also Black 1986, and DeLong, Shleifer, Summers, and Waldmann 1990). Noise traders are different from liquidity traders in that they trade based on false information while believing that they have access to superior information. For example, when informed insiders are buying, noise traders who are falsely informed as to the extent that the price has already reflected the inside information, sell their shares to informed traders at a small premium above the market price. This resolves the adverse selection problem of the market maker who can broker the transaction between informed and falsely informed traders rather than trading directly with the informed traders.

A total of 38 insiders bought 265,600 shares in the insider trading period of June 30, 1982, through August 2, 1982. This amounts to 29% of Campbell Taggart's volume in the period of insider trading and 121% of the volume in March 1982, three months before the leak. The share price increased from the premerger price of $23.25 on June 1, to the acquisition price of $38 per share, representing a premium of 63%. The results also show that volume increased significantly both during and after the merger announcement. The increase in volume represents trading by both the insiders and uninformed traders. Finally, the data show little change in the bid-ask spread during the insider trading period, disputing the arguments of the theoretical literature.

In sum the Cornell-Sirri paper provides strong evidence to reject the notion that liquidity is reduced and bid-ask spreads are widened due to insider trading.

Arguments in Favor of Insider Trading

Financial Market Equilibrium

In financial markets information asymmetry among market participants leads to speculative buy and sell activities. There are at least three equilibrium hypotheses that explain these activities. The strong form of the efficient market hypothesis (Fama 1970) contends that market prices reflect both public and private information. Access to private information does not improve the performance of trading since market prices have reflected such information. In this model private information is redundant. In contrast, the competitive equilibrium hypothesis (Debreu 1959) postulates that traders use private information but do not extract information from market prices. Under the noisy rational expectations equilibrium (Grossman and Stiglitz 1980) the trader makes decisions based on both private information and price.

The test of these hypotheses revolves around noise traders versus informed traders. Friedman (1953), Fama (1965), and Black (1986) argue that irrational investors (noise traders) trade based on false information (noise) that they believe to be true. Rational arbitragers (informed investors) trade against noise traders and help to bring prices to their fundamental values. According to this argument, noise traders will lose over time to arbitragers and eventually disappear from the market.

De Long, Shleifer, Summers, and Waldmann (1990), however, disagree with this contention. They argue that since arbitragers generally have short-term horizons, they may have to liquidate their positions before noise traders' beliefs revert to their mean. In the meantime, the disparity between the fundamental values according to the informed trader and the price due to trading by noise traders may widen. Unless informed traders wait for a long time before liquidating their positions, they may lose to noise traders in the short run. The aversion to fundamental risk further complicates the trading position of the arbitragers even if they extend their horizon (Campbell and Kyle 1987).

Lang, Litzenberger, and Madrigal (1992) provide an empirical test of competing financial market equilibrium hypotheses. The test is based on stock market trading volume where each hypothesis imposes a different set of restrictions on the correlation between volume, prices, and the expectational variables. The results are consistent with the noisy rational expectations model. The other hypotheses are rejected. The noisy rational expectations model predicts that when there is high variance in noise trading the traders will rely heavily on their private information and less on the price. Conversely, when there is low variance in noise trading, then the actions of informed traders directly affect the price. This implies a strong private incentive to acquire information beyond what is already reflected on the price (inside information).

To the extent that noise traders affect share prices based on their false information, the capital allocation process becomes less efficient. A process that would provide genuine information to the market will revert the prices to their true values. Production and dissemination of inside information provides this solution. Cornell and Sirri (1992) demonstrate empirically how insider trading offsets noise trading, leaving market makers unharmed. The concerns shown in the theoretical research regarding widening of bid-ask spreads and reduction of liquidity do not seem to occur simply because market makers match the trades of informed insiders with that of the noise trader without having to bear the risk themselves. In short, the existing evidence indicates that trading by informed investors drives financial markets to equilibrium.

Globalization of the Economy, Advancements in Technology, and Incompatibility of Insider Trading Regulations

While anti-insider trading regulations have been part of the securities laws in the United States for more than half a century, their enforcement reached a new plateau in 1986 when the SEC and the Department of Justice brought charges against a large number of traders and their respective firms. During the same period most other industrialized nations either did not have any rules against insider trading or they simply did not enforce them. While this trend seems to have changed in the past few years, no other country has yet to develop as extensive a set of laws and case precedents as the United States.

Before the 1980s, most European countries did not prohibit insider trading. Limited restrictions on insider trading existed in Great Britain, Germany, Luxembourg, and The Netherlands. France was an exception, having adopted anti-insider trading laws in the 1970s. Lemieux (1991) reports that these changes in the 1980s were largely a result of pressures imposed by U.S. authorities on the regulators of these industrialized nations. For example, Great Britain adopted insider trading legislation in 1980, Sweden and Norway in 1985, Denmark in 1986, Greece and Spain in 1988, The Netherlands, Belgium, and Ireland in 1989, and Portugal in 1991. In 1989, the European community required its members to adopt uniform insider trading legislation by June 1, 1992, on which only Germany has yet to comply. The movement in the industrialized countries of Europe and Asia towards a uniform regulated system regarding insider trading has yet to reach the magnitude and the reach of such legislation in the United States. The outlook does not guarantee that they ever will.

The advancements in information technology through sophisticated computers with capacity to collect, process, and exchange information at significant speed enables rapid dissemination of information worldwide. With various stock exchanges being open in different time zones and a large number of stocks being listed in multiple international exchanges, there is a 24-hour market for a large number of securities. If information containment, insider trading rules, and the enforcement activities vary from country to country, nonpublic information will be disseminated first in the least regulated of the markets and then will be transferred to other markets by its reflection on the share prices.

In the United States the original laws against insider trading were passed when information technology was in its relative infancy, and the international communications and information exchange channels were at significantly less developed stages. While the transaction cost rationale for incorporating insider trading rules within the corporate law as opposed to a set of voluntary contracts may have been justifiable at the time, advancements in technology and the development of international market interlinks have altered such parameters significantly. Such market-based changes will ultimately make outdated regulations obsolete. This will not be cost-free, however. In the meantime, the government agencies will unevenly enforce the law by targeting certain groups and by relying on selective prosecutions. This seems to have taken place in the past decade where selective individuals and firms were prosecuted primarily through tips and heavy-handed use of RICO laws. The empirical inquiry, however, shows that this effort has not reduced the extent of insider trading, albeit the pattern of trading has changed from registered insiders to outside-insiders.

As the economy is integrated globally, competition among various countries will intensify significantly. The governments that impose the most restrictive set of rules may end up losing the economic competition. Less regulated countries will attract and retain the business from their more regulated competitors. This may ultimately induce the governments of more regulated countries to reconsider their rules. But the lag in regulatory reform will be very costly for such economies.

Internally Produced Information: Property Rights, Fiduciary Duties, and Contractual Agreements in the Usage of Inside Information

If inside information is produced within the firm, it may be argued that the property rights to that information belong to the residual claimants or equity holders. Officers, board members, and to a lesser extent outside accountants, attorneys, and investment advisors to the firm carry fiduciary duties towards shareholders. If shareholders determine that inside information has the highest value to them they can include in their contractual agreements with their fiduciaries provisions that will explicitly prohibit the use of inside information in their trading. If any of the parties violate the contractual provision, administrative or legal actions could be taken to remedy the problem. Termination of employee contracts, expulsion of directors from the board, discontinuation of legal or investment advisory services are examples of administrative responses to the violation of explicit contractual provisions that prohibit insider trading. Legal rules may also be used to enforce contracts. However, if shareholders decide that property rights should be assigned to managers as part of their compensation contract, they should have the right to do so.

Externally Produced Information: The Role of Third Tier Brokerage Houses

Currently, there are two tiers of brokerage houses: the discount brokerage houses that fill the buy and sell orders of clients without financial advice; and full-service brokerage houses that provide financial advice based on publicly available information. If insider trading is decriminalized, there will be an opportunity to set up a third tier brokerage business that will use not only publicly available information but will also actively produce inside information for its clientele. The effectiveness of the *Wall Street Journal's* Heard on the Street column in affecting share prices is a good example of how material nonpublic information is produced externally. Third tier brokerage houses can produce such information and openly advertise its sale to prospective clients. This will provide another alternative for investors in their choice of brokerage services.

Plausibility of externally produced material nonpublic information in the context of a brokerage house may defuse some of the criticisms waged against insider trading from the point of view of equity and fairness. It is fair and equitable because it provides an opportunity for every shareholder to have access to information that is not widely distributed. Information production technology will help in bringing market prices closer to their true values and will diminish noise trading.

Policy Implications and Conclusions

The weight of evidence examined in this book indicates that attempts to eliminate insider trading via legislation have failed. Specifically, regulation has caused insider trading to be shifted from registered insiders to temporary and outside-insiders. As a result, we contend that the current regulatory policies overcriminalize insider trading. Therefore, we advocate their reconsideration.

There are two factors that have contributed to sustained insider trading despite regulation. First, trading based on material nonpublic information is very profitable, while the probability of detection for all but registered insiders is quite small. Outsiders, may obtain valuable information in a variety of ways and transact on such information with very little likelihood of being caught. Identifying such traders who have no disclosure or fiduciary responsibilities is a difficult task. Second, the Supreme Court has provided inconsistent opinions on the liabilities of outside-insiders. This has left market professionals and their attorneys to find loopholes that would allow them to side-step the anti-insider trading laws. Further, the high number of out-of-court settlements in recent years is suggestive of inadequate and/or inappropriate regulatory policies. The volume of settlements can be attributed to two related factors. First, because of the ambiguities in the existing anti-insider trading laws state and Federal courts have differed in interpreting the laws. This makes it difficult to prosecute the indicted cases successfully in court. Second, many out-of-court settlements of recent years were attained due to threat of indictment under RICO. In recent years, however, courts have been overturning RICO indictments. The publicity regarding the abuse of RICO laws has provided an impetus for further legislation by Congress to limit its application. Currently, prosecutors have a more difficult time indicting the accused inside traders under RICO. And if defendants are no longer threatened by RICO indictments, there likely will be less cooperation with authorities and it will be more difficult to detect outside-insider trading. Finally, despite a significant increase in the extent of anti-insider trading legislation, empirical evidence indicates that insider trading has continued (and perhaps increased) in recent years. Thus, the stated regulatory objective to promote equity in marketplace has not been achieved while millions of dollars have been expended in vain.

To continue the pattern of additional regulation is a doomed strategy. The only real solution is to reconsider the rationale, the intended targets of the policies, and the potential for the regulations to achieve their intended goals. We contend that equity in trading would be better served by decriminalization of insider trading. This policy would enable organized brokerage houses and securities firms to collect inside information legally for their clients for a fee. Investors have the option of purchasing such service. Currently, clients of full service brokerage houses are charged for analysis of the information in financial statements and annual reports of publicly traded firms.

Thus, legalization of insider trading introduces at least four benefits. First, it generates another line of information production and revenue source for the organized investment houses. Second, it provides an opportunity for ordinary investors to share in trading based on inside

information. Third, the process ultimately will lead to fa
efficient dissemination of information. And fourth, decrin
the process will reduce the burden on judicial systems and
limited time to concentrate on more socially beneficial cas

REFERENCES

Admati, A.R., and P. Pfleiderer. (1988). "A Theory of Industry Patterns, Volume and Price Variability," *Review of Financial Studies* Vol. 1, pp. 3—40.

Agrawal, A., and G. Mandelker. (1990). "Large Shareholders and the Monitoring of Managers: The Case of Antitakeover Charter Amendments," *Journal of Financial and Quantitative Analysis* Vol. 25, pp. 143—161.

Alchian, A. A., and H. Demsetz. (1973). "Property Rights Paradigm," *Journal of Economic History* Vol. 33, pp. 16—27.

Arshadi, N., and T. H. Eyssell. (1991). "Regulatory Deterrence and Registered Insider Trading: The Case of Tender Offers," *Financial Management* Vol. 20, pp. 30—39.

Arshadi, N., T. H. Eyssell, K. L. Kempf. (forthcoming). "The Law and Finance of Corporate Insider Trading," *Financial Practice and Education*.

Asquith, P., and E. H. Kim. (1982). "The Impact of Merger Bids On the Participating Firms' Security Holders," *Journal of Finance* Vol. 37, pp. 1209—1228.

Asquith, P., D. Mullins, and E. Wolff. (1989). "Original Issue High Yield Bonds: Aging Analysis of Defaults, Exchanges, and Calls," *Journal of Finance* Vol. 44, pp. 923—952.

Auerbach, A., and D. Reishus. (1988). "The Effects of Taxation on Merger Decisions," in *Corporate Takeovers: Causes and Consequences*, A. Auerbach (ed.) Chicago, Illinois: University of Chicago Press, pp. 157—183.

Baesel, J. B., and G. R. Stein. (1979). "The Value of Information: Inferences from the Profitability of Insider Trading," *Journal of Financial and Quantitative Analysis* Vol. 14, pp.553-571.

Bagehot, W. (1989). "The Only Game in Town," *Financial Analysts Journal* Vol. 22, pp. 12—14.

Baker, G., M. Jensen, and K. Murphy. (1988). "Compensation and Incentives: Practice vs. Theory," *Journal of Finance* Vol. 43 pp. 593—616.

Bamber, L. S. (1986). "The Information Content of Annual Earnings Releases: A Trading Volume Approach," *Journal of Accounting Research* Vol. 24, pp. 40-56.

Beatty, R., and J. Ritter. (1987). "Investment Banking, Reputation, and the Underpricing of Initial Public Offerings," *Journal of Financial Economics* Vol. 15, pp. 213—232.

Benesh, G. A., and R. A. Pari. (1987). "Performance of Stocks Recommended on the Basis of Insider Trading Activity," *The Financial Review* Vol. 22, pp. 145—158.

Benston, G. (1973). "Required Disclosure and the stock Market," *American Economic Review* Vol. 63, pp. 132—155.

Berle A., and G. Means. (1932). *The Modern Corporation and Private Property*. New York: Macmillan Publishing.

Black, Fisher. (1986). "Noise," *Journal of Finance* Vol. 41, pp. 529—543.

Blackwell, D., M. Marr, and M. Spivey. (1990). "Shelf Registration and the Reduced Due Diligence Argument: Implications of the Underwriter Certification and the Implicit Insurance Hypothesis," *Journal of Financial and Quantitative Analysis* Vol 25, pp. 245—259.

Booth, J., and R. Smith. (1986). "Capital Raising, Underwriting, and the Certification Hypothesis," *Journal of Financial Economics* Vol. 15, pp. 261—281.

Brick, I. E., M. Statman, and D. G. Weaver. (1989). "Event Studies and Model Misspecification: Another Look at the Benefits of Outsiders From Public Information About Insider Trading," *Journal of Business, Finance, and Accounting* Vol. 16, pp. 399—424.

Brickley, J., and F. Dark. (1987). "The Choice of Organizational Form: The Case of Franchising," *Journal of Financial Economics* Vol. 16, pp. 401—420.

Brickley, J., R. Lease, and C. Smith. (1988). "Ownership Structure and Voting on Antitakeover Amendments," *Journal of Financial Economics* Vol. 17, pp. 267—291.

Brodsky, E., and R. P. Swanson. (1988). "Insider Trading Litigation: The Obstacles to Recovery," *Securities Regulation Law Journal* Vol. 16, pp. 31-53.

Brown, S., and J. Warner. (1980). "Measuring Security Price Information," *Journal of Financial Economics* Vol. 8, pp. 205-258.

Brown, S., and J. Warner. (1985). "Using Daily Stock Returns: The Case of Event Studies," *Journal of Financial Economics* Vol. 14, pp. 1-31.

Brown, K. C., and M. V. Raymond. (1986). "Risk Arbitrage and the Prediction of Successful Corporate Takeovers," *Financial Management* Vol. 15, pp.54—63.

Brown, C., and J. Medoff. (1988). "The Impact of Firm Acquisitions on Labor," *Corporate Takeovers: Causes and Consequences,* A. Auerbach, (ed.) Chicago, Illinois: University of Chicago Press, pp. 9—28.

Brown, S. J., and J. B. Warner. (1980). "Measuring Security Price Information," *Journal of Financial Economics* Vol. 8, pp. 205—258.

Brudney, V. (1979). "Insiders, Outsiders, and Informational Advantages under the Federal Securities Laws," *Harvard Law Review* Vol. 93, pp. 322—376.

Campbell, J. Y., and A. Kyle. (1987). "Smart Money, Noise Trading, and Stock Price Behavior," Manuscript, Princeton, N. J.: Princeton University.

Carlton, D. W., and D. R. Fischel. (1983). "The Regulation of Insider Trading," *Stanford Law Review* Vol. 35, pp. 857—95.

Carney, W. J. (1987). "Signalling and Causation in Insider Trading," *Catholic University Law Review* Vol. 36, pp. 863—898.

Casey, W. (1972). "The Securities Bar and The Securities Laws," in *Addresses at Annual Meeting of Banking, Corporation and Business Law Section of N. Y. Stat Bar Association* (Jan. 27), p. 19.

Chalk, A., and J. Peavy, III. (1985). "Understanding the Pricing of Initial Public Offerings," *Research in Finance* Vol. 8, pp. 203—240.

Cleeton, D. L., and P. A. Reeder. (1987). "Stock and Option Markets: Are Insider Trading Regulations Effective?," *Quarterly Review of Economics and Business* Vol. 27, pp. 63—76.

Coase, R. (1937). "The Nature of the Firm," *Economica* Vol. 4 pp. 386—405.

Coase, R. H. (1960). "The Problem of Social Cost," *Journal of Law and Economics* Vol. 3, pp. 1—44.

Coase, R. (1988). *The Firm, the Market, and the Law*, Chicago, Illinois: The University of Chicago Press.

Cohen, L. R. (1990). "Why Tender Offers? The Efficient Market Hypothesis, the Supply of Stocks, and Signaling," *The Journal of Legal Studies* Vol. 19, pp. 113-143.

Cohen, S. S. (1991). "The Death of Securities Regulation," *The Wall Street Journal* January 17, p. A10.

Copeland, T., and D. Galai. (1983). "Information Effects on the Bid—Ask Spread," *Journal of Finance* Vol. 38, pp. 1457—1469.

Cornell, B., and E. R. Sirri. (1992). "The Reaction of Investors and Stock Prices to Insider Trading," *Journal of Finance* Vol. 47, pp. 1031—1059.

Cox, J. D. (1986). "Insider Trading and Contracting: A Critical Response to the Chicago School," *Duke Law Journal* Vol. 1986, pp. 628—659.

Dahlman, C. (1979). "The Problem of Externality," *The Journal of Law and Economics* Vol. 23, p. 148.

DeAngelo, H., and L. DeAngelo. (1989). "Proxy Contests and the Governance of Publicly Held Corporations," *Journal of Financial Economics* Vol. 18, pp. 29—59.

Debreu, G. (1959). *Theory of Value: An Axiomatic Analysis of Economic Equilibrium*, New Haven, Conn.: Yale University Press.

De Long, J. B., A. Shleifer, L. H. Summers, and R. J. Waldmann. (1990). "Noise Trader Risk in Financial Markets," *Journal of Political Economy* Vol. 98, pp. 703—738.

Demsetz, H. (1967). "Towards a Theory of Property Rights," *American Economic Review* Vol. 57, pp. 347—359.

Denis, D. (1991). "Shelf Registration and the Market for Seasoned Equity Offerings," *Journal of Business* Vol. 64, pp. 189—212.

Dennis, D., and J. McConnell. (1986). "Corporate Mergers and Security Returns," *Journal of Financial Economics* Vol. 15, pp. 143—187.

Diamond, D. W., and R. E. Verrecchia. (1981). "Information Aggregation in a Noisy Rational Expectations Economy," *Journal of Financial Economic* Vol. 9, pp. 221—235.

Dodd, P., and R. S. Ruback. (1977). "Tender Offers and Stockholder Returns: An Empirical Analysis," *Journal of Financial Economics* Vol. 5, pp. 351—373.

Dooley, M. P. (1980). "Enforcement of Insider Trading Restrictions," *Virginia Law Review* Vol. 66, pp. 1—83.

Dye, R. A. (1984). "Inside Trading and Incentives," *Journal of Business* Vol. 57, pp. 295—312.

Easley, D., and M. O'Hara. (1987). "Price, Trade Size, and Information in Securities Markets," *Journal of Financial Economics* Vol. 19, pp. 69—90.

Easterbrook, F. H. (1981). "Insider Trading, Secret Agents, Evidentiary Privileges, and the Production of Information," *The Supreme Court Review* pp. 309—365.

Easterbrook, F., and D. Fischel. (1991). *The Economic Structure of Corporate Law,* Cambridge, Massachusetts: Harvard University Press.

Elliot, J., D. Morse, and G. Richardson, (1984). "The Association Between Insider Trading and Information Announcements," *Rand Journal of Economics* Vol. 15, pp. 521-536.

Eyssell, T. H. (1990). "Corporate Insiders, Toehold Acquisitions, and Information Leakage: Do Insiders Tip Their Hands?," *Akron Business and Economic Review* Vol. 21, pp. 90—103.

Eyssell, T. H. (1991). "Corporate Insiders and the Death of the Firm: Evidence on the Incidence of Insider Trading in Corporate Dissolutions," *Financial Review* Vol. 26, pp. 517—534.

Eyssell, T. H., and N. Arshadi. (1993). "Insiders, Outsiders, or Trend—Chasers? An Investigation of Pre—Takeover Transactions in the Shares of Target Firms," *Journal of Financial Research* Vol 16. pp. 49—59.

Eyssell, T. H., and J. Reburn. (1993). "The Effects of the Insider Trading Sanctions Act of 1984: The Case of Seasoned Equity Offerings," *Journal of Financial Research* Vol 16, pp. 163—172.

Eyssell, T. H., and D. Kummer. (forthcoming). "Signalling, Insider Trading, and Post–Offering Performance: The Case of Initial Public Offerings," *Journal of Applied Business Research*.

Fama, E. F. (1965). "The Behavior of Stock Market Prices," *Journal of Business* Vol. 38, pp. 34—105.

Fama, E. (1970). "Efficient Capital Markets: A Review of Theory and Empirical Work," *Journal of Finance* Vol 23, pp. 383—417.

Fama, E. (1980). "Agency Problems and the Theory of the Firm," *Journal of Political Economy* Vol. 88, pp. 288—307.

Fama, E. (1985). "What's Different About Banks," *Journal of Monetary Economics* Vol. 13, pp. 29—39.

Fama, E. (1991). "Efficient Capital Markets: II," *Journal of Finance* Vol. 46, pp. 1575—1617.

Fama, E., and M. Jensen. (1983a). "Separation of Ownership and Control," *Journal of Law and Economics* Vol. 26, pp. 301—325.

Fama, E., and K. French. (1988). "Permanent and Temporary Components of Stock Prices," *Journal of Political Economy* Vol. 96, pp. 246—273.

Fama, E., and M. Jensen. (1983b). "Agency Problems and Residual Claims," *Journal of Law and Economics* Vol. 26, pp. 327—349.

Fama, E., L. Fisher, M. Jensen, and R. Roll. (1969). "The Adjustment of Stock Prices to New Information," *International Economic Review* Vol. 10, pp. 1—21.

Finnerty, J. E. (1976a). "Insiders and Market Efficiency," *Journal of Finance* Vol. 31, pp. 1141—1148.

Finnerty, J. E. (1976b). "Insiders' Activity and Inside Information: A Multivariate Analysis," *Journal of Financial and Quantitative Analysis* Vol. 11, pp. 205—216.

Franks, J., and R. Harris. (1989). "Shareholder Wealth Effects of Corporate Takeovers: The U.K. Experience 1955—1985," *Journal of Financial Economics* Vol. 18 pp. 225—249.

Friedman, M. (1953). "The Case for Flexible Exchange Rates," *Essays in Positive Economics,* Chicago: University of Chicago Press.

Friedman, L. M. (1985). *A History of American Law.* 2d ed. New York: Simon & Schuster.

Gammill, J. F., E. R. Sirri, and M. Fleming. (1992). "Liquidity, Efficiency, and Profitability Surrounding Delayed Openings and Trading Halts on the NYSE," Working Paper, Harvard Business School.

Garten, H. A. (1987). "Insider Trading in the Corporate Interest," *Wisconsin Law Review* Vol. 68, pp. 573-640.

Gilson, R. (1986). *The Law and Finance of Corporate Acquisitions.* New York: Foundation Press.

Gilson, S. (1988). "Optimal Capital Structure and Management—Borne Cost of Financial Distress," Unpublished Manuscript, University of Rochester, N.Y.

Glosten, L. R., and P. R. Milgrom. (1985). "Bid, Ask and Transaction Prices in a Specialist Market with Heterogeneously Informed Traders," *Journal of Financial Economics* Vol. 14, pp. 71—100.

Glosten, L. R. (1989). "Insider Trading, Liquidity, and the Role of the Monopolist Specialist," *Journal of Business* Vol. 62, pp. 211—235.

Goldie, R. (1983). "The Inside Edge: A Study of Insider Trading in Canada," *Business Review* pp. 67—72.

Goldie, R., and K. Ambachtsheer. (1983). "Are Some Insiders More 'Inside' Than Others? Comment.," *Journal of Portfolio Management* Vol. 10, p. 75.

Gordon, H. S. (1954). "The Economic Theory of a Common Property Resource: The Fishery," *Journal of Political Economy* Vol. 62, pp. 124—142.

Gosnell, T., A. J. Keown, and J. M. Pinkerton. (1992). "Bankruptcy and Insider Trading: Differences Between Exchange—Listed and OTC Firms," *Journal of Finance* Vol. 47, pp. 349—362.

Grossman, S. J., and J. E. Stiglitz. (1980). "On the Impossibility of Informationally Efficient Markets," *American Economic Review* Vol. 70, pp. 393—408.

Guest, A. G. (1961). ed. *Oxford Essays in Jurisprudence (First Series).* Oxford: Clarendon Press.

Gupta, A., and L. Misra. (1988). "Illegal Insider Trading: Is It Rampant Before Corporate Takeovers?," *Financial Review* Vol. 23, pp. 453—464.

Haddock, D. D., and J. R. Macey. (1987). "Regulation on Demand: A Private Interest Model, with an Application to Insider Trading Regulation," *The Journal of Law and Economics* Vol. 30, pp. 311-352.

Haft, R. J. (1982). "The Effect of Insider Trading Rules on the Internal Efficiency of the Large Corporation," *Michigan Law Review* Vol. 80, pp. 1051—1071.

Harris, L. E. (1986). "A Transaction Data Survey of Weekly and Intraday Patterns in Stock Returns," *Journal of Financial Economics* Vol. 16, pp. 71—100.

Hasbrouck, J. (1988). "Trades, Quotes, Inventories and Information," *Journal of Financial Economics* Vol. 22, pp. 229—252.

Haw, I., V. S. Pastena, and S. B. Lilien. (1990). "Market Manifestation of Nonpublic Information Prior to Mergers: The Effect of Ownership Structure," *The Accounting Review* Vol. 65, pp. 432—451.

Heller, H. (1982). "Chiarella, SEC Rule 14e—3 and Dirks: 'Fairness' Versus Economic Theory," *The Business Lawyer* Vol. 37, pp. 517—558.

Herman, E. (1981). *Corporate Control, Corporate Power.* Cambridge: Cambridge University Press.

Herzel, L., and L. Katz. (1987). "Insider Trading: Who Loses?," *Lloyds Bank Review* pp. 15—26.

Hilke, J. (1984). "Early Mandatory Disclosure Regulations," *FTC Working Paper* No. 111.

Hirschey, M., and J. Zaima. (1989). "Insider Trading, Ownership Structure, and the Market Assessment of Corporate Sell—Offs," *Journal of Finance* Vol. 44, pp. 971—980.

Hirschey, M., M. B. Slovin, and J. K. Zaima. (1990). "Bank Debt, Insider Trading, and the Return to Corporate Selloffs," *Journal of Banking and Finance* Vol. 14, pp. 85-98.

Holderness, C., and D. P. Sheehan. (1985). "Raiders or Saviors? The Evidence on Six Controversial Investors," *Journal of Financial Economics* Vol. 14, pp. 555—579.

Ibbotson, R. (1975). "Price Performance of Common Stock New Issues," *Journal of Financial Economics* Vol. 2, pp. 235—272.

Ibbotson, R., and J. Jaffe. (1975). "'Hot Issues' Markets," *Journal of Finance* Vol. 30, pp. 1027—1042.

Jaffe, J. (1974a). "Special Information and Insider Trading," *Journal of Business* Vol. 47, pp. 410-428.

Jaffe, J. (1974b). "The Effect of Regulation Changes on Insider Trading," *Bell Journal of Economics and Management Science* Vol. 5, pp. 93-121.

James, C. (1987). "Some Evidence on the Uniqueness of Bank Loans," *Journal of Financial Economics* Vol. 19, pp. 217—235.

Janvey R. S. (1986). "SEC Investigation of Insider Trading," *Securities Regulation Law Journal* Vol. 13, pp. 299—331.

Janvey R. S. (1987). "Criminal Prosecution of Insider Trading," *Securities Regulation Law Journal* Vol. 15, pp. 136—153.

Jarrell, G. (1981). "The Economic Effects of Federal Regulation of the Market for New Securities Issues," *Journal of Law and Economics* Vol. 24, pp. 613—675.

Jarrell, G., and M. Bradley. (1980). "The Economic Effects of Federal and State Regulation of Cash Tender Offers," *Journal of Law and Economics* Vol. 23, pp. 371—388.

Jarrell, G. A., and A. B. Poulsen. (1989a). "Stock Trading Before the Announcement of Tender Offers: Insider Trading or Market Anticipation?," *Journal of Law, Economics, and Organization* Vol. 5, pp. 225—248.

Jarrell, G., and A. Poulsen. (1989b). "The Returns to Acquiring Firms in Tender Offers: Evidence From Three Decades," *Financial Management* Vol. 18, pp. 12—19.

Jarrell, G., J. Brickley, and G. Netter. (1988). "The Market for Corporate Control: The Empirical Evidence Since 1980," *Journal of Economic Perspectives* Vol. 2, pp. 49—68.

Jensen, M., and R. Ruback. (1983). "The Market for Corporate Control: The Scientific Evidence," *Journal of Financial Economics* Vol. 12, pp. 5—50.

Jensen, M., and J. Zimmerman. (1985). "Management Compensation and the Managerial Labor Market," *Journal of Accounting and Economics* Vol 1, pp. 3—9.

John, K., and L. H. P. Lang. (1991). "Insider Trading Around Dividend Announcements: Theory and Evidence," *Journal of Finance* Vol. 46, pp. 1361—1389.

Karjala, D. S. (1982). "Statutory Regulation of Insider Trading in Impersonal Markets," *Duke Law Journal* September, pp. 627—649.

Karpoff, J. M., and D. Lee. (1991). "Insider Trading Before New Issue Announcements," *Financial Management* Vol. 20, pp. 18—26.

Keown, A. J., and J. M. Pinkerton. (1981). "Merger Announcements and Insider Trading Activity: An Empirical Investigation," *Journal of Finance* Vol. 36, pp. 855—869.

Keown, A. J., and J. M. Pinkerton, L. Young, and R. S. Hansen. (1985). "Recent SEC Prosecution and Insider Trading on Forthcoming Merger Announcements," *Journal of Business Research* Vol. 13, pp. 329—337.

Kerr, H. S. (1980). "The Battle of Insider Trading vs. Market Efficiency," *Journal of Portfolio Management* Vol. 6, pp. 47—50.

King, R., and T. O'Keefe. (1986). "Lobbying Activities and Insider Trading," *The Accounting Review* Vol. 61, pp. 76-90.

Klein, B. (1980). "Transaction Cost Determinants of "Unfair" Contractual Arrangements," *American Economic Review* Vol. 70, pp. 356—362.

Klein, B., and K. Laffler. (1981). "The Role of Market Forces in Assuring Contractual Performance," *Journal of Political Economy* Vol. 89, p. 615—641.

Kyle, A. S. (1985). "Continuous Auctions and Insider Trading," *Econometrica* Vol. 53, pp. 1315—1335.

Lang, L. H. P., R. H. Litzenberger, and V. Madrigal. (1992). "Testing Financial Market Equilibrium under Asymmetric Information," *Journal of Political Economy* Vol. 100, pp. 317—348.

Langevoort, D. C. (1992). "Theories, Assumptions, and Securities Regulation: Market Efficiency Revisited," *University of Pennsylvania Law Review* Vol. 140, pp. 851—920.

Larcker, D. F., R. E. Reder, and D. T. Simon. (1983). "Trades By Insiders as Evidence of the Existence of Economic Consequences of Accounting Standards," *The Accounting Review* Vol. 58, pp. 606—620.

Larcker D. F., and Lys T. (1987). "An Empirical Analysis of the Incentives to Engage in Costly Information Acquisitions: The Case of Risk Arbitrage," *Journal of Financial Economics* Vol. 18, pp. 111-126.

Lee, M. H., and H. Bishara. (1989). "Recent Canadian Experience on the Profitability of Insider Trades," *The Financial Review* Vol. 24, pp. 235—249.

Leftwich, R. (1981). "Evidence of the Impact of Mandatory Changes in Accounting Principles on Corporate Loan Agreements," *Journal of Accounting and Economics* Vol. 3, pp. 3-36.

Leland, H. E. (1992). "Insider Trading: Should It Be Prohibited?," *Journal of Political Economy* Vol. 100, pp. 859—887.

Leland, H. E., and D. H. Pyle. (1977). "Informational Asymmetries, Financial Structure, and Financial Intermediation," *Journal of Finance* Vol. 32, pp. 371—387.

Lemieux, P. (1991). *Apologie des Sorcieres Modernes.* Paris: Les Belles Lettres.

Leroy, S., and R. Porter. (1981). "Stock Price Volatility: Tests Based on Implied Variance Bounds," *Econometrica* Vol. 49, pp. 555—574.

Lin, J., and J. S. Howe. (1990). "Insider Trading in the OTC Market," *Journal of Finance* Vol. 45, pp. 1273—1284.

Loderer, C., and D. P. Sheehan. (1989). "Corporate Bankruptcy and Managers' Self—Serving Behavior," *Journal of Finance* Vol. 44, pp. 1059—1075.

Lorie, J. H., and V. Niederhoffer. (1968). "Predictive and Statistical Properties of Insider Trading," *Journal of Law and Economics* Vol. 11, pp. 35-51.

Magenheim, E., and D. Mueller. (1988). "Are Acquiring Firm Shareholders Better Off After an Acquisition?," *Corporate Takeovers: Causes and Consequences,* A. Auerbach, (ed.) Chicago, Illinois: University of Chicago Press, pp. 171—193.

Malkiel, B. (1987). "Efficient Market Hypothesis," in *The New Palgrave: A Dictionary of Economics*. J. Eatwell, M. Milgate, and P. Newman, (eds.), London: The Macmillan Press, Vol. 2, pp. 120—123.

Mankiw, N., D. Romer, and M. Shapiro. (1991). "Stock Market Forecastability and Volatility: A Statistical Appraisal," *Review of Financial Studies* Vol. 4, pp. 455—478.

Manne, H. (1965). "Mergers and the Market for Corporate Control," *Journal of Political Economy* Vol. 73, pp. 110-120.

Manne, H. (1966). *Insider Trading and the Stock Market*. New York: Free Press.

Manne, H. (1966). "In Defense of Insider Trading," *Harvard Business Review* Vol. 44, pp. 113—122.

Manne, H. (1967). "Our Two Corporation Systems: Law and Economics," *Virginia Law Review*, pp. 259—285.

Martin, K. (1986). "Firm Performance and Managerial Discipline in Contests for Corporate Control," Working Paper, Purdue University.

Masse, I., R. Hanrahan, and J. Kushner. (1991). "Takeover Related Insider Trading in Different Legislative Jurisdictions," *Journal of the Midwest Finance Association* Vol. 20, pp. 107—113.

Mayers, D., and C. Smith, Jr. (1981). "Contractual Provisions, Organizational Structure, and Conflict Control in Insurance Markets," *Journal of Business* Vol. 54, pp. 407-434.

Mayers, D., and C. Smith, Jr. (1987). "Corporate Insurance and the Underinvestment problem," *Journal of Risk and Insurance* Vol. 54, pp.45-54.

McGee, R. W. (1988). "Insider Trading: An Economic and Philosophical Analysis," *The Mid—Atlantic Journal of Business* Vol. 25, pp. 35—47.

Meulbroek, L. (1992). "An Empirical Analysis of Illegal Insider Trading," *Journal of Finance* Vol. 47, pp. 1661—1700.

Mikkelson, W., and R. S. Ruback. (1985). "An Empirical Analysis of the Interfirm Equity Investment Process," *Journal of Financial Economics* Vol. 14, pp. 523—553.

Mikkelson, W., and M. Partch. (1986). "Valuation Effects of Security Offerings and the Issuance Process," *Journal of Financial Economics* Vol. 15, pp. 31—60.

Mitchell, M., and K. Lehn. (1990). "Do Bad Bidders Make Good Targets?," *Journal of Applied Corporate Finance* Vol. 3, pp. 60-69.

Morck, R., A. Shleifer and R. Vishny. (1988). "Management Ownership and Market Valuation," *Journal of Financial Economics* Vol. 17, pp. 293—315.

Morck, R., A. Shleifer, and R. Vishny. (1990). "Do Managerial Objectives Drive Bad Acquisitions?" *Journal of Finance* Vol. 45, pp. 31—48.

Morse, D. (1981). "Price and Trading Vol. Reaction Surrounding Earnings Announcements: A Closer Examination," *Journal of Accounting Research* Vol. 19, pp. 374-383.

Myers, S., and N. Majluf. (1984). "Corporate Financing and Investment Decisions When Firms Have Information That Investors Do Not Have," *Journal of Financial Economics* Vol. 13, pp. 187—221.

Nathan, K., and T. O'Keefe. (1989). "The Rise in Takeover Premiums," *Journal of Financial Economics* Vol. 18, pp. 101—119.

Netter, J. M., and M. L. Mitchell. (1989) "Stock—Repurchase Announcements and Insider Transactions After the October 1987 Stock Market Crash," *Financial Management* Vol. 18, pp. 84—96.

Nozick, R. (1974). *Anarchy, State, and Utopia*. New York: Basic Books.

Nunn, K. P., G. P. Madden, and M. J. Gombola. (1983). "Are Some Insiders More 'Inside' Than Others?," *Journal of Portfolio Management* Vol. 9, pp. 18—22.

Odaiyappa, R., and S. M. Khalid Nainar. (1992). "Economic Consequences of SFAS No. 33—An Insider Trading Perspective," *The Accounting Review* Vol. 67, pp. 599—609.

Palepu, K. G. (1986). "Predictive Takeover Targets: A Methodological and Empirical Analysis," *Journal of Accounting and Economics* Vol. 8, pp. 3-37.

Peltzman, S. (1976). "Toward a More General Theory of Regulation," *Journal of Law and Economics* Vol. 19, pp. 211—240.

Penman, S. H. (1982). "Insider Trading and the Dissemination of Firms' Forecast Information," *Journal of Business* Vol. 55, pp. 479—503.

Penman, S. H. (1985). "A Comparison of the Information Content of Insider Trading and Management Earnings Forecasts," *Journal of Financial and Quantitative Analysis* Vol. 20, pp. 1—17.

Pincus, M. (1983). "Information Characteristics of Earnings Announcements and Stock Market Behavior," *Journal of Accounting Research* Vol. 21, pp. 155-183.

Pope, P.F., R.C. Morris, and D.A. Peel. (1990). "Insider Trading: Some Evidence on Market Efficiency and Directors' Share Dealings in Great Britain," *Journal of Business, Finance, and, Accounting* Vol. 17, pp. 359—380.

Posner, R. (1971). "Taxation by Regulation," *Bell Journal of Economics and Management Science* Vol. 2, pp. 22—50.

Pound, J., and R. Zeckhauser. (1990). "Clearly Heard on the Street: The Effect of Takeover Rumors on Stock Prices," *Journal of Business* Vol. 63, pp. 291—308.

Pratt, S. P., and C. W. DeVere. (1978). "Relationship Between Insider Trading and Rates of Return for NYSE Common Stocks, 1960—66," in *Modern Developments in Investment Management*. James Lorie and Richard Brealey, (eds.) Hinsdale, Illinois: The Dryden Press.

Prentice, R. A. (1987). *Law of Business Organization and Securities Regulation*. Englewood Cliffs: Prentice Hall.

Ratner, D. (1988). *Securities Regulations*. St. Paul, Minnesota: West Publishing Company.

Richardson, G., S. Sefcik, and R. Thompson. (1986). "A Test of Dividend Irrelevance Using Volume Reactions to a Change in Dividend Policy," *Journal of Financial Economics* Vol. 17, pp. 313-333.

Ritter, J. (1984). "The 'Hot Issue' Market of 1980," *Journal of Business* Vol. 57, pp. 215—240.

Ritter, J. (1985). "The Choice Between Firm Commitment and Best Effort Contracts," Unpublished Working Paper, U. of Pennsylvania, Philadelphia, PA.

Rogoff, D. I. (1964). "The Forecasting Properties of Insiders' Transactions," Unpublished D.B.A. dissertation, Michigan State University.

Rozeff, M. S. (1987). "Insider Trading: What We Know and What We Don't Know," in W. M. Hollman, R. Frederick, and E. Petry Jr., (ed.), *The Effects of Organizational Transformation*, New York: Quorum Books.

Rozeff, M., and M. Zaman. (1988). "Market Efficiency and Insider Trading: New Evidence," *Journal of Business* Vol. 61, pp. 25—44.

Ryngaert, M., and J. Netter. (1987). "Shareholder Wealth Effects of the Ohio Antitakeover Law," Working Paper.

Sanders, R. W., and J. S. Zdanowicz. (1992). "Target Firm Abnormal Returns and Trading Volume Around the Initiation of Change—in—Control Transactions," *Journal of Financial and Quantitative Analysis* Vol. 27, pp. 109-129.

Scott, K. E. (1980). "Insider Trading, Rule 10b—5, Disclosure and Corporate Privacy," *Journal of Legal Studies* Vol. 9, pp. 801—818.

Seyhun, H. (1986). "Insiders' Profits, Costs of Trading, and Market Efficiency," *Journal of Financial Economics* Vol. 16, pp. 189—212.

Seyhun, N. (1988). "The January Effect and Aggregate Insider Trading," *Journal of Finance* Vol. 43, pp. 129—141.

Seyhun, N. (1988). "The Information Content of Aggregate Insider Trading," *Journal of Business* Vol. 61, pp. 1-24.

Seyhun, N. (1990a). "Do Bidder Managers Knowingly Pay Too Much for Target Firms?," *Journal of Business* Vol. 63, pp. 439—464.

Seyhun, N. (1990b). "Overreaction or Fundamentals: Some Lessons From Insiders' Responses to the Market Crash of 1987," *Journal of Finance* Vol. 45, pp. 1363—1388.

Seyhun, H. (1992). "The Effectiveness of the Insider Trading Sanctions," *Journal of Law and Economics* Vol. 35, pp. 149—182.

Shiller, R. (1981). "Do Stock Prices Move Too Much to be Justified by Subsequent Changes in Dividends?" *American Economic Review* Vol. 71, pp. 421—436.

Shleifer A., and L. Summers. (1988). "Breach of Trust in Hostile Takeovers," in *Corporate Takeovers: Causes and Consequences.* A. Auerbach, ed., Chicago, Illinois: University of Chicago Press, pp. 33—56.

Shleifer A., and R. Vishny. (1986). "Large Shareholders and Corporate Control," *Journal of Political Economy* Vol. 94, pp. 461—488.

Shubik, M. (1985). "Corporate Control, Efficient Markets, the Public Good, the Law and Economic Theory and Advice," Working Paper Series F, Yale University School of Management .

Silver, C. B. (1985). "Penalizing Insider Trading: A Critical Assessment of the Insider Trading Sanctions Act of 1984," *Duke Law Journal* Vol. 1985, pp. 960—1025.

Simkowitz, M., and R. J. Monroe. (1971). "A Discriminate Analysis Function for Conglomerate Targets," *Southern Journal of Business* Vol. 6, pp. 1-16.

Simon, C. (1989). "The Effect of the 1933 Securities Act on Investor Information and the Performance of New Issues," *The American Economic Review* Vol. 79, pp. 295—318.

Sirri, E. R. (1991). "Price, Volume, and Bid—Ask Spread in a Specialist Market," Working Paper, Harvard Business School.

Smiley R. (1981). "The Effects of State Securities Statutes on Tender Offer Activity," *Economic Inquiry* Vol. 19, pp. 426—435.

Smith, F. P. (1941). Management Trading, Stock—Market Prices, and Profits. Cambridge: Yale University Press.

Smith, C., and J. Warner. (1979). "On Financial Contracting: An Analysis of Bond Covenants," *Journal of Financial Economics* Vol. 7, pp. 117—161.

Stevens, D. L. (1973). "Financial Characteristics of Merged Firms: A Multivariate Analysis," *Journal of Financial and Quantitative Analysis* Vol. 8, pp. 149-165.

Stewart, J. (1991). *Den of Thieves*. New York: Simon and Schuster.

Stigler, G. (1964). "Public Regulation of the Securities Markets," *Journal of Business* Vol. 37, pp. 117—142.

Stigler, G. (1971). "The Theory of Economic Regulation," *The Bell Journal of Economics and Management Science* Vol. 2, pp. 3—21.

Trivoli, G. W. (1980). "How to Profit From Insider Trading Information," *Journal of Portfolio Management* Vol. 6, pp. 51—56.

Walsh, J. (1988). "Top Management Turnover Following Mergers and Acquisitions," *Strategic Management Journal* Vol. 9, pp. 173—183.

Warner, J., R. Watts, and K. Wruck. (1988). "Stock Prices and Top Management Changes," *Journal of Financial Economics* Vol. 17, pp. 461—492.

Weinberger, A. M. (1990). "Preventing Insider Trading Violations: A Survey of Corporate Compliance Programs," *Securities Regulation Law Journal* Vol. 18, pp. 180—193.

Weisback, M. (1988). "Outside Directors and CEO Turnover," *Journal of Financial Economics* Vol. 17, pp. 431—460.

Winans, R. F. (1986). *Trading Secrets*. New York: St. Martin's Press.

Wu, H. (1964). "Corporate Insider Trading in the Stock Market," *National Banking Review* Vol. 2, pp. 373—385.

INDEX